Space, Politics and Aesthetics

Series Editors: Alex Thomson, Benjamin Arditi, Andrew Schaap
International Advisory Editors: Michael Dillon, Michael J. Shapiro, Jeremy Valentine

Offering New Perspectives on Contemporary Political Theory, books in this series 'take on' the political in accordance with the ambivalent colloquial sense of the phrase – as both an acceptance and a challenge. They interrogate received accounts of the relationship between political thought and political practice, criticise and engage with the contemporary political imagination, and reflect on the ongoing transformations of politics. Concise and polemical, the texts are oriented towards critique, developments in Continental thought, and the crossing of disciplinary borders.

Titles in the *Taking on the Political* series include:

www.euppublishing.com/series/totp

Space, Politics and Aesthetics

Mustafa Dikeç

EDINBURGH
University Press

Edinburgh University Press is one of the leading university presses in the UK. We publish academic books and journals in our selected subject areas across the humanities and social sciences, combining cutting-edge scholarship with high editorial and production values to produce academic works of lasting importance. For more information visit our website: www.edinburghuniversitypress.com

Edinburgh University Press Ltd
The Tun – Holyrood Road
12(2f) Jackson's Entry
Edinburgh EH8 8PJ

Typeset in 11 on 13 Sabon by
Iolaire Typesetting, Newtonmore

First published in hardback by Edinburgh University Press 2015

A CIP record for this book is available from the British Library

ISBN 978 0 7486 8597 4 (hardback)
ISBN 978 0 7486 8598 1 (paperback)
ISBN 978 0 7486 8599 8 (webready PDF)
ISBN 978 0 7486 8601 8 (epub)

Contents

Acknowledgements

The writing of this book has been a collective process during which I have incurred many debts. It was a pleasure to work with the series editors, Benjamin Arditi, Andrew Schaap and Alex Thomson, whose encouragement, patience and generosity made the long process of writing and rewriting not only inspiring, but enjoyable as well. If readers find any interesting ideas in this book, I can assure them that they owe much to the editors' constructive remarks, and the faults and weaknesses to my inability to address them effectively.

Over the years I have been lucky to have had the chance to discuss my ideas about politics and space with wonderful teachers, colleagues and friends. For their generosity, I am grateful to John Allen, Guy Baeten, Clive Barnett, Julie-Anne Boudreau, Tim Cresswell, Felix Driver, Stuart Elden, Dave Featherstone, Matthew Gandy, Liette Gilbert, Derek Gregory, Maria Kaika, David Lambert, Carina Listerborn, Alex Loftus, Jeff Malpas, Doreen Massey, Kirstie McClure, Walter Nicholls, Steve Pile, Raymond Rocco, Ove Sernhede, Ed Soja, Erik Swyngedouw and Catharina Thörn. Not all of them would agree with the ideas presented in this book, but such is the nature of academic enterprise.

Nicola Ramsey, Michelle Houston, Rebecca Mackenzie and Edward Clark at Edinburgh University Press have been very helpful, and patiently answered my many questions. It was a pleasure to work with Hilary Walford and Eliza Wright during the copy-editing process. I thank all of them for making this process go as smoothly as possible.

None of the chapters of this book reproduces a previously published article in its entirety. However, parts of three previously published articles have found their way in to the book: 'Space, Politics, and the Political', *Environment and Planning D: Society and Space*, 23/2 (2005), 171–88; 'Politics is Sublime', *Environment and Planning D: Society and Space*, 30/2 (2012), 262–79 (Pion Ltd, London, www. pion.co.uk, www.envplan.com, www.societyandspace.com); and 'Beginners and Equals: Political Subjectivity in Arendt and Rancière', *Transactions of the Institute of British Geographers*, 38/1(2013), 78–90. I thank these journals and publishers for allowing me to use material from these articles.

The last word must go to my family. Without their love and support, I would not have been able to complete this project, or, even if I had, it would not have been half as enjoyable as it has. For their love, and the many wondrous everyday delights and challenges that come with it, I thank Claire, Joakim, Elif and Félix. And Aslan is missed, never forgotten.

Mustafa Dikeç
Paris, September 2014

For Claire, with love and gratitude

Chapter 1
Politics and the Spatial Imagination

Space as a Mode of Political Thinking

This book explores the spatial and aesthetic dimensions of politics. What interests me in particular is the theoretical work space does for conceptualisations of politics. Focusing on the work of Hannah Arendt, Jean-Luc Nancy and Jacques Rancière, I pay attention to what animates them in engaging with space in theorising politics. Why does space have such a strong appeal in their theories? What does their recourse to spatial terms tell us about the nature of politics and space as they conceive them? Attending to the spatial aspects of their conceptualisation of politics allows me to discern their central spatial assumptions and paradigms, and to consider what 'space' theoretically does for them. None of them equates space with politics in a straightforward manner, but their conceptualisation of politics, in their different ways, implies some form of generative spatial rupture in the established order of things, creating new relations and connections. Politics inaugurates space, and spatialisation is central to politics as a constitutive part of it.

This emphasis on space connects to the main argument of the book: that politics is about forms of perceiving the world and modes of relating to it. How this world is constructed, disclosed and disrupted is a matter of politics. Making sense of the world requires aesthetic forms, 'aesthetic' understood as perception by the senses (*aisthesis*), rather than matters of art and beauty. Space not only gives form to and orders how this world appears, but also allows distinctive gatherings of beings – things and people – that establish relationality and open new spaces. This implies an understanding of space as a form and mode of apprehending the world and worldly relations, departing from a conception of space as something already given, a background for relations between things, a fixed and inert 'container'. Space becomes a form of appearance and a mode of actuality, making manifest established orders, generating particular relationships to them, and providing relational domains of experience for the constitution of political identities.

This way of conceiving space brings us close to the Kantian notion of '*a priori* forms' that order our sensory perceptions. In the *Critique of Pure Reason*, Kant defined space and time as *a priori* forms of intuition or sensibility. As *a priori* forms, space and time make objects possible and organise the multitude of sensations we receive into a whole, and thus give form to our experience of the world. We encounter particular objects, and become aware of them as spatially (and temporally) ordered – as exhibiting relations of simultaneity and succession – and as having a form – possessing spatial features such as shape and extension. According to Kant, this spatial (and temporal) system of relations is *a priori* and has its source in our minds; namely, our faculty of spatial intuition, or our 'outer sense', as he also refers to it. That it is *a priori* means, however, that it is already given to us, built in our minds, that it does not rely on experience, but merely gives form to our awareness of things in space (and time).

The Kantian version suggests a capacity for spatial bringing-together, which is politically promising in that it allows for the possibility of relating and ordering what we perceive. But what gives space form? If space is a sensible manifestation of things, what is it that makes some things spatially manifest but not others? While recognising the political potential of a capacity for spatially relating and bringing things together, it seems to me important also to problematise what space gives form to and to conceive it as the product of particular historical and geographical contexts. What do we gain politically if we admit that space cannot be reduced to mere immutable forms and their juxtapositions?

Lefebvre, Marxist philosopher and theorist of social production of space, once wrote: 'I repeat that there is a politics of space, because space is political' (*il y a politique de l'espace parce que l'espace est politique*) (Lefebvre 1977: 345).[1] What is translated as 'politics of space' (*politique de l'espace*) also means 'spatial policy', as, for example, conceived by the state. Lefebvre is critical of state policies for treating space as an objective and neutral medium that can be unproblematically organised through policy-making and technical expertise, but does not deny such uses. There is an untranslatable play on words in the statement *l'espace est politique*, which could mean 'space is policy', 'space is political', as well as 'space is politics'. As a product of social relations, rather than an inert background for them, space is contested and imbued with tension. It is neither naturally given nor immutable, but rather a product of interrelations always in the making, and thus both disrupted and a source of disruption (Massey 1999). This dynamism and the contested nature of space offer transformative possibilities, which renders it 'political'.

But space is not 'political' in a univocal sense. It is as much about inauguration of politics as it is about its containment; it is as much about openings as it is about closings; it is as much ruptural as it is governmental. To take one example, the series of urban revolts since 2000 showed how people act from the material conditions of their spaces – from what gives space form – seeking alternative distributions or organisations – seeking to give space form. In doing so, they make and occupy spaces, making space give form to their grievances, demands and solidarity. These spatialisations give political actors a sense of empowerment, but also create governmental anxieties, because they make spatially manifest what was perhaps not evident before, and give rise to new forms and modes of perceiving the world and relating to it. This is why urban revolts include a central element of contestation in and over space (what should or should not be made spatially manifest; what and who should give space form). These spatialisations are also instances of thinking politics spatially, which I take to be significant for actors as well as for theorists of politics who act and think with a certain vision.

Vision, Wolin notes, can be understood in two ways: as an act of perception and as an act of imagination. Politics as vision brings together these descriptive and imaginative elements. Political thinking is 'a form of "seeing" political phenomena', but political thinkers also rely on imagination as a 'necessary element in theorizing' (Wolin 2004: 17, 19). The imaginative element in political thinking allows for the abstraction of certain phenomena and establishing connections between them, rendering intelligible a myriad of practices and processes that cannot be fully 'known'. This imaginative reordering of political life requires the employment of concepts and categories to draw implications from practices and processes, and to bring out connections between them that are not self-evident from observable facts.

Space, I argue, is one such category in political thinking and theorising. Political thinking brings together a disposition to be moved by and a capacity to relate and order what we perceive. Spatial imagination – seeing connections that cannot always be deduced rationally from the givens, establishing new relations and gatherings, envisaging new forms and configurations – is thus an important part of political thinking. This capacity to bring things into spatial (and temporal) relationship is also an essential part of how we apprehend the world in so far as we apprehend things spatially as having a form (possessing spatial features such as shape and extension), and as ordered (exhibiting relations of simultaneity). This makes space politically significant because spatialisation is fundamental to constructing, apprehending and projecting worlds and entering into relation with them.

Thinking politics spatially is both figurative, in the sense that it evokes spatial forms, and imaginative, which allows for the possibility of reordering things. As Zerilli (2005: 59) argues, 'the capacity to create forms or figures that are not already given in sensible experience or the order of concepts' allows for the possibility of disrupting and altering established orders and systems of representation. As we will see, Arendt, Nancy and Rancière are committed to an understanding of politics that is ruptural and inaugurative, by which I mean a politics that starts or introduces something new and interrupts the established order of things. This aspect is also evident in their refusal to conceive politics around already given identities or interests. They all mobilise a rich spatial vocabulary, and there is a strong and widespread appeal to spatial terms in their conceptualisation of politics. This book shows that their use of spatial terms is not arbitrary; they all make certain propositions, implicit or explicit, about space. Theirs is a mode of thinking that makes spatial formations, orders, distributions and relations integral parts of politics. For each, politics implies some form of generative spatial rupture in the established order of things, creating new relations, orders and meanings. This is what I call 'space as a mode of political thinking'.[2] But how is this spatial aspect related to the aesthetic dimension of their politics?

Political Aesthetic

I use the term 'political aesthetic' to refer to the aesthetic premises that underlie the political thinking of Arendt, Nancy and Rancière. Their conceptualisation of politics has an important aesthetic dimension in that it depends on the construction and apprehension of worlds through spatial forms and distributions. Having a form, exhibiting relations of simultaneity and order are essential for their politics to work. Space performs this aesthetic function by giving form and order to objects of perception; it is a capacity for things to appear and exhibit relations of simultaneity and order. But space, as we have seen above, is not neutral; the production of space is contested and conflictual in so far as social relations and spatial formations are mutually constitutive. If we maintain that space cannot be reduced to mere immutable forms and their juxtapositions, and that it is about processes as well, then space takes on a dynamic, transformative and conflictual quality; politically problematic, but also replete with political possibilities.[3] As we will see in the following chapters, it is precisely when they take space and its production unproblematically that these thinkers, Arendt and Nancy in particular, end up with a problematic understanding of politics.

The term 'political aesthetic' is also a reminder of these thinkers' debt to Kant's aesthetic theory as developed in his third Critique, the *Critique of Judgment*.[4] Even though this seems an unlikely place for thinkers of ruptural and inaugurative politics to look for inspiration, Arendt, Nancy and Rancière all find something politically appealing and innovative in Kant's aesthetics, but appropriate different elements of it. Arendt focuses on common sense, Nancy on 'presentation' (*Darstellung*) and Rancière on 'equality'. Thus, political aesthetic is central to both the connections and differences between these three thinkers of politics. There is, however, a risk involved in such an endeavour, as illustrated by Jay's review (1992) of what 'aesthetic' and 'aestheticised politics' may mean.[5] The connotations of aestheticised politics that come out of his review are not gratifying: 'irrationality, illusion, fantasy, myth, sensual seduction, the imposition of will, and inhumane indifference to ethical, religious, or cognitive considerations' (Jay 1992: 45). As he observes, Benjamin's association of fascism with the introduction of aesthetics into politics has led to the establishment of a firm link between 'the aestheticisation of politics' and fascism. But the link between aesthetics and politics is not necessarily evil. Jay (1992: 51) notes that there are other implications of aestheticising politics rather than 'hastily turning all aesthetic politics into a prolegomenon to tyranny'.[6] In other words, the relationship between aesthetics and politics is not limited to what Mitchell (2013: 115) calls 'Benjamin's fatal choice between fascism and communism'.

As we will see, the politics of Arendt, Nancy and Rancière are far from the form of aestheticised politics that Walter Benjamin associated with fascism. They converge on mobilising notions from Kant's aesthetic theory in their political theorising, but differ in what they mobilise. They also converge on giving space a fundamental role for the construction of worlds of sensory experience, and making some form of spatialisation constitutive of their politics. The deployment of spatial figures provides them with a perceptually rich domain, and allows them to define a locus for politics, while avoiding its confinement in already established institutions. Space thus allows them to account for the specificity of politics. Such spatial differentiation is not always unproblematic, as we will see especially with Arendt. Nevertheless, the deployment of spatial figures allows them to grapple with different issues and dilemmas. Some form of spatialisation is necessary for the constitution of common worlds, which is central to their politics, and for the inauguration of politics as an activity that is neither confined to nor exhausted by institutional spaces.

Although all three make space part of their conceptualisation of politics, they differ in their spatial premises. Among the three, as I will argue, only Rancière's spatial premises allow for a consideration of the conflictual and problematic nature of spatialisation as a political problem, and for a recognition of the historical and geographical contingency of spatial formations and configurations. Arendt and Nancy also make spatialisation constitutive of their politics, but they tend to take space as an unproblematic category when they use it merely as a tool of demarcation. Even though they also suggest that space is not pre-given but produced through encounters with others, their conceptualisation of politics does not problematise the production of space in the inauguration of politics.

Despite their differences, however, Arendt, Nancy and Rancière share an aversion to the idea that 'everything is political', which comes down to saying that nothing is. This is partly why they all try, in their own way, to define the specificity of politics, which requires distinguishing what they see as specifically political. As we will see, they all conceive of politics as different and distinct from institutionalised practices of government and administration. Nancy, in his earlier writings, distinguishes 'politics' (*la politique*), associated with established practices of government and administration, from 'the political' (*le politique*). Rancière distinguishes, in a similar vein, between what he calls 'the police', a term he uses to refer to established orders of governance, and 'politics', implying a disruptive episode. Arendt goes even further and argues for a specific realm for politics, not to be contaminated by social or private matters. All three agree that what they see as properly political cannot be restricted to institutionalised practices, even if such practices may formally define the sphere of 'politics'. But in this attempt to define the specificity of politics they run a risk: while trying to avoid one unhelpful extreme – 'everything is political' – they are threatened with the other – 'purity of politics'. An understanding of politics with its own specific logic, form of activity or realm even inevitably leads to concerns about a purist attempt to 'save' politics in its alleged specificity from its banal, everyday operations in municipal buildings, government offices or polling stations.

How, then, are we to interpret this attempt? There may be good reasons to criticise attempts to 'purify' politics. However, I will risk a more generous interpretation of the 'specificity of the political' thesis in so far as it distinguishes politics from institutionalised practices of government and administration. The aim of this distinction, as I understand it, is less to distinguish the 'purely' or 'properly' political (however defined) from the non-political than to keep the possibility for politics open by insisting that anything can become a matter of politics – and anyone a political subject – without having to be granted official approval or even recognition (as we will see with the *sans papiers* in Chapter 3). This is significant in that it avoids a possible illusion that the established institutions and spaces of politics, however democratic, will suffice to address all political wrongs and exhaust all political possibilities.[7] An emphasis on politics as some form of spatialisation – the opening-up of new spaces – establishes politics as different and distinct from already consolidated formations and arrangements, while recognising that politics is neither unrelated to nor immune from them. Politics exceeds established spaces, practices and procedures, but it does not occur *ex nihilo*, and it needs, as Arendt in particular recognised, the security and stability granted by them.[8]

Therefore, I am more tempted to see the attempt of these thinkers as a helpful reminder of this political excess rather than as a naive and futile attempt to define the purely and properly political. The eruptions of the past few years around the world may be taken as a sign of this, although not all of them took place in democratic regimes. But, even if we look at the liberal democracies of the West since the beginning of the twenty-first century, in this age of 'urban

rage' (Dikeç, forthcoming), we see an unprecedented wave of uprisings, spectacular urban demonstrations and revolts, which were
repressed by an increasingly militarised police. This suggests that
contemporary processes (economic, urban, political) produce forms
of dissent that the established institutions of liberal democracies
cannot accommodate in uncoercive ways. There is, in other words,
something that eludes the established and formal spaces of these
democracies, an excess that keeps breaking out. What animates me
in engaging with these thinkers, then, is not a worry that things are
not properly political any more, but the fact that an excess keeps
erupting. These thinkers open new ways of thinking about this excess
in political terms, rather than as matters of social order, criminology,
policing or government.

Since the three thinkers I am engaging with share a debt to Kant for
their political aesthetic, I start with an explication of their particular
interpretations of Kant's aesthetics for their politics in Chapter 2.
Taking inspiration from different elements of Kant's aesthetics as
developed in his third Critique, Arendt, Nancy and Rancière suggest,
I argue, a political relation to the world that is not one of knowing, but one of aesthetics. Arendt saw Kant's third Critique as his
'unwritten' political philosophy. She finds it politically appealing
for its notion of aesthetic judgement that is free from the limitations
of rational norms and criteria, which suits her particularly well as a
political thinker who adamantly resists conceiving of politics around
given standards and rules or truth claims that compel agreement.
Kant's notion of aesthetic judgement not only liberates her from the
rigidity of truth claims, rules and standards, but also allows her to
conceive the creation of common worlds through uncoerced assent
with an appeal to common sense. Judgement thus becomes a world-
making practice in Arendt's political aesthetic based on the creation
of common worlds through a plurality of encounters.

The freedom Arendt finds in Kant resonates with Nancy as well,
because his ontology rejects any originary or given meaning. Nancy
emphasises the creation of meaning through sharing, and identifies
what he calls 'the space of sharing' with the political. He appropriates
the notion of presentation from Kant, which implies aesthetic forms
and worldliness. Presentation, I argue, is a key theme for Nancy
because, on the one hand, it makes possible worldly engagement
and engagement with the world in freedom – free from pre-given
conceptual determinations, as Kant's notion of aesthetic judgement

demands. On the other, it avoids everything becoming pure multiplicity; we are free from conceptual determination, yet are still able to experience the empirical world by giving form to those things with which we are presented.

A central theme in both Arendt's and Nancy's politics, then, is the constitution and disclosure of the common: a shared space as a common domain of experience, or, as Nancy would have put it, as experience 'in-common'. The common is also a significant theme in Rancière, but he puts emphasis on its disruption. His political aesthetic does not appeal to common sense, as Arendt's does, but implies a disruption of 'common sense' – of what is commonly made available to the senses and made to make sense. He does not focus on presentation, as Nancy does, but spatialisation, understood as the appearance of sensible orders, is central to his political aesthetic. He is inspired by Kant's notion of aesthetic judgement, although his concern is not on judging as such, but on what making a judgement implies. I argue that, through an unorthodox interpretation of Kant's first and third Critiques, Rancière establishes a relationship between aesthetics, equality and dissensus that is central to his conceptualisation of politics.

Despite these differences, what unites these thinkers is that their political aesthetic requires space and spatialisation. The 'common', its constitution, disclosure and disruption, is central to their politics, and this is why space, as a form and mode of apprehending the common, is central to their thinking. Their conceptualisation of politics relies on the apprehension of the world through aesthetic forms and the construction of a shared and relational domain of experience, where space as a form of appearance and mode of actuality becomes central, though in different ways. While the central spatial paradigm in Arendt and Nancy is a distinctive coming-together, it is distribution in Rancière. In Chapter 3, I explore Arendt's understanding of action and her spatial premises. Political action, for Arendt, inaugurates space – her 'space of appearance' – where individuals are at once related and separated. This spatialisation, I argue, is a sensible manifestation of the freedom of the acting subject. It is also a medium, creating an order of relations between and a shared domain of experience for individuals in their distinctiveness and plurality. For Arendt, politics needs a 'stage' for both actors and spectators, for public appearance is an integral part of it. Spatialisation provides this space of encounter as a domain for mutual exposure and relationality.

Appearance and mutual exposure are also central to Nancy's politics, as Chapter 4 shows. Politics, for Nancy, implies altering a given order of meanings by opening new spaces of mutual exposure in and through which meaning 'in-common' can be produced. Rather than privileging established institutions, Nancy thus puts emphasis on the creation of new spaces. For Nancy, the political implies inauguration of space in and through which the very structuring principles of the community, which is always in the making, are put into question. This space is a place of 'being-in-common', a notion that Nancy uses to imply that there are no definitive bases for attachment – in other words, no proper places that definitively secure identities. The space inaugurated by the political is itself inaugural where freedom is exercised, which, in Nancy's thought, has a spatial quality. Nancy's ontology relies on the contingent creation of sense through relations 'in-between', the 'where' of which is provided by space. Finding meaning requires aesthetic forms, and this is why he finds Kant's notion of presentation appealing, because it suggests making sense of aesthetic forms in their freedom; that is, in the absence of concepts that determine them.

For Nancy, then, sense is presented through sensible forms. Rancière as well puts emphasis on our experience of the sensible world and the way we make sense of it, as we will see in Chapter 5. To accept established orders, or to be moved by our experience of them, to contest and challenge them are matters of sensory experience for Rancière. His conceptualisation of politics implies a relationship between aesthetic forms – as objects of sensory perception – and established orders of hierarchy and domination. Such orders are apprehended through spatial forms and distributions; they are, indeed, based on framings of space (and time) – what he calls the 'distribution of the sensible'. Space, this chapter shows, performs this function as a form of appearance and a mode of actuality. For Rancière, forms of governance are consolidated and apprehended spatially (and temporally), and he is concerned with the forms of inequality such orders create. Politics takes place within consolidated orders by introducing a spatial rupture. A spatial perspective makes it clear that established governing orders ('the police', in his vocabulary) and politics are enmeshed, and Rancière is very careful with his use of spatial terms here, especially with the distinction between 'space' (*espace*) and 'place' (*lieu*), on the one hand, and 'place' (*place*), on the other, which gets lost in English translation.

Enactments of equality inaugurate space, making it the place where a wrong can be addressed and equality be demonstrated.

The idea of spatial rupture is what leads to my association of politics with the aesthetic features of the Kantian sublime, as something that defeats our senses and disrupts our ways of sensing and making sense of the world. In the final chapter, then, I argue that the disruption of our forms of perceiving the world and modes of relating to it is the sublime element in politics. Arendt, Nancy and Rancière, as I read them, all argue for a scrutiny of established orders and practices that constitute our common worlds. Their politics is disruptive in that they invite us to stop-and-think, as Arendt would have put it. This reflective withdrawal from the accepted givens, normalised practices and repetitive structures of everyday life, within which we tend to get caught up, has political value as it allows us to engage with the world in a more reflexive, rather than habitual, mode. This is why I associate politics with the aesthetic features of the sublime, because it unsettles our routinised ways of sensing and making sense of the world by introducing an element that cannot initially find a register in our habitual spatial orderings. Politics implies a disruption of our habitual ways of sensing and making sense of the world, although a disruption does not necessarily imply 'good' politics. Totalitarian regimes, fascist governments, military coups also radically disrupt our ways of knowing and relating to the world. In evoking the image of the sublime, therefore, I do not advance an unconditional espousal of disruptive and transformative politics for the sake of disruption and transformation. I also make clear that my association of the image of the sublime with politics is not meant to transform sublime unrepresentability into an ethical imperative of absolute respect for otherness (as in Lyotard), but rather to emphasise the point that political subjects do not exist *qua* political subjects before they introduce a rupture in the established order.

Chapter 2
Politics of Aesthetics

Castella, the Factory-Owner

Castella has a big moustache and he tells vulgar jokes. He does not like reading, he does not like the theatre. He spends his days at a factory, which belongs to him, and his evenings at the theatre, to which he seemingly does not belong. His unrefined ways, lack of education and artistic culture make him an object of ridicule when he joins the artists for dinner after the spectacle, with the hope of gaining the sympathy of the lead actress, Clara, with whom he has fallen madly in love.

But they seem worlds apart. Castella's efforts seem merely to consolidate his position as a joking matter in this artistic milieu. In yet another attempt to be close to Clara, Castella attends an exhibition by one of her painter friends, and buys a painting. But how could this moustachioed industrialist have a taste for painting not induced by some other motivation? The painter's boyfriend believes that Castella felt obliged to buy the painting after having unwittingly insulted him and the painter with a pejorative remark on gays. Clara thinks Castella is buying art to impress her. But Castella goes even further: he commissions the painter to paint a mural on the façade of his factory, which happens to be a paint factory.

Although the painter believes that Castella has commissioned the painter because he appreciates his art, and therefore sees no harm in their agreement, Clara is convinced that they are taking advantage of his feelings towards her. 'I know Castella,' she says; 'he doesn't appreciate it. He doesn't *know* a thing.' But when she visits the factory to put an end to this exploitation, as she sees it, Castella surprises her by telling her that he actually likes the paintings, and that is why he is buying them. 'You didn't think for a minute it could be because I liked them? Don't worry,' he assures Clara, 'it's because I like them'.

Clara is speechless; even this uneducated, vulgar factory-owner – who does not *know*, as she had said, a thing – has taste. He is not, as she wrongly assumed, trying to satisfy 'the taste of others' – the film's title[1] – but rather trying to satisfy his own. There is something egalitarian here: Castella is capable of making judgements of taste, just like her, her painter friend and all the others.

What political lessons can be drawn from this story? There is one obvious route to take, following Bourdieu to read this as a critique of taste. We would then see poor Castella as humiliated and oppressed because of his lack of taste, which is the result of his lack of education, cultural capital and so on. This would then imply a politics that would expose and denounce all grantors and grounds for privilege (elite schools, cultural and institutional structures), and in this sense it would be an egalitarian politics with equality as its objective. This is a fine politics, but it denies all capacity to Castella. In this scenario, he can only play the role of 'poor Castella' – indeed, he has to remain only that for the critique to have any legitimacy at all. If there is any hope for emancipation for our poor Castella, it will come from the critic's denunciation of markers of privilege and distinction.

Can we make Castella play a different role – a part where he emancipates himself by demonstrating a capacity that is denied to him? Can we engage with Castella in his – and our –   freedom without confining him to the role of the vulgar industrialist, and accept that he has taste and is capable of making aesthetic judgements? The conceptualisations of politics explored in this book demand that we answer these questions in the affirmative. In what follows, I will show on what basis we could do so, and how taste and aesthetic judgement may inspire political thinking. I will argue that Arendt, Nancy and Rancière offer instances of an aesthetic mode of political thinking that is not constructed around epistemological justification, knowledge or truth claims, or means–end calculation. This is not to suggest that what are taken as fact or truth, or interests and objectives, are irrelevant for politics; they certainly are, but they are not what is specific to politics. These thinkers suggest a political relation to the world that is not one of knowing, but one of aesthetics, and I am interested in the political implications of such an aesthetic orientation.[2]

It is also this aesthetic orientation, I will suggest, that makes space and spatialisation important for these thinkers – that makes space a mode of political thinking. The political aesthetic of Arendt, Nancy and Rancière – the aesthetic premises that underlie their political thinking – has its sources in a strand of aesthetic theory that does not reduce aesthetics to matters of art and beauty. Central to the political aesthetic of all three is *aisthesis*: without apprehension and revelation, without a form of presentation and a domain of relationality, their politics would not work. Space performs this aesthetic function for them by giving form and order to objects of perception, and by allowing for distinctive gatherings and relationality.

Arendt, Nancy and Rancière all find something politically appealing in Kant's writings on taste and aesthetic judgement, rather than in his work on practical reason, which was the basis for Kant's own political philosophy. 'Behind taste, a favourite topic of the whole eighteenth century,' Arendt (1992: 10) writes, 'Kant discovered an entirely new human faculty, namely, judgement'. It is this 'faculty' that attracts them to Kant's writings on aesthetics in his third Critique, the *Critique of Judgment*, though for different reasons. Arendt and Nancy both find Kant's liberation of aesthetic judgement from rational norms and criteria politically inspiring. Arendt also adopts aesthetic judgement's implications of communicability and sociability for thinking plurality, which she saw as an essential condition of politics. If we shared merely a capacity for action, communicability and the construction of common worlds, as Arendt understood those, would not be possible. The idea of a 'common sense' that follows from a shared capacity for judgement helps Arendt address this problem. She develops a political aesthetic that emphasises an appeal to common sense (in its Kantian version) for the creation of common worlds in a context of plurality. Kant's notion of aesthetic judgement allows her to relate plurality, communicability and worldliness, all of which are integral elements of her conception of the public realm – what she calls the 'space of appearance'.

The idea of the creation and disclosure of a common world is also prominent in Nancy's understanding of politics. The Kantian inspiration is evident in his commitment to the idea of an engagement with the world in freedom, making sense of what is presented to us without pre-given determinations. Spatialisation gives form to and relates beings in the constitution and disclosure of common worlds. Rancière's politics, on the other hand, implies a disruption of common sense, of what is commonly made available to the senses and made to make sense. Like Arendt, Rancière is also inspired by Kant's postulate that aesthetic judgement is something we equally share. Unlike her, however, he does not focus on what this implies for communicability. This postulate signals, for Rancière, an egalitarian politics where equality is taken as a given rather than as an objective to be attained. His emphasis is not on judging as such, but on what making – being capable of making – a judgement implies. We are less interested in Castella's judgement (Does he like the painting? Does he not?) than in his verification of a shared capacity. Even he, who does not 'know a thing', is capable of making aesthetic judgements. Rancière makes this postulate of equality central to his politics, and develops a political aesthetic around forms of perceiving the world and modes of relating to it. His concern, as we will see, is to locate moments when equality is 'wronged' by the consolidation of spatial and temporal orders or verified by the opening-up of new spaces.

In order to understand the role space plays in the political thinking of Arendt, Nancy and Rancière, it is first necessary to get a clear sense of their political aesthetic. Since they all share a debt to Kant for their political aesthetic, I start with an overview of Kant's notion of aesthetic judgement, and ask what the relevance of aesthetic judgement may be for thinking politics. I then focus on Arendt, Nancy and Rancière, showing how each interpreted and adopted Kant in their particular ways – Arendt focusing on common sense, Nancy on presentation, and Rancière on equality. This allows me to define their political aesthetic and the role space plays in it. As we will see, perception by the senses – *aisthesis* – is central to their political aesthetic, and the constitution and disclosure of the common are a main theme in their conceptualisations.

Aesthetic Judgement and Common Sense

In the first Critique, *Critique of Pure Reason*, Kant defines judgement as 'the faculty of subsuming under rules, i.e., of determining whether something stands under a given rule . . . or not' (A133/B172). Without this faculty, without, that is, concepts with which to classify particulars, we cannot have knowledge. But not all judgements are the same, and Kant provides a distinction in his third Critique, the *Critique of Judgment* (CJ):

> The power of judgement in general is the faculty for thinking of the particular as contained under the universal. If the universal (the rule, the principle, the law) is given, then the power of judgement, which subsumes the particular under it, ... is *determining*. If, however, only the particular is given, for which the universal is to be found, then the power of judgement is merely *reflecting*. (*CJ*, Introduction, section IV)[3]

Kant thus distinguishes between two kinds of judgement, 'reflective' and 'determinative'. Aesthetic judgements (or judgements of taste) are reflective judgements. What distinguishes them from determinative judgements is that they proceed without a concept. Since reflective judgements are made in the absence of (or free from) concepts, they do not contribute to knowledge:

> The judgement of taste is therefore not a cognitive judgement, hence not a logical one, but is rather aesthetic, by which is understood one whose determining ground cannot be other than subjective. Any relation of representations, however, even that of sensations, can be objective ... but not the relation to the feeling of pleasure and displeasure, by means of which nothing at all in the object is designated, but in which the subject feels itself as it is affected by the representation. (*CJ* §1)[4]

Here we may pause for a while to consider a few questions. What makes such judgements 'aesthetic', understood as relating to the sensible aspect of our experience? How could an aesthetic judgement be detached from the object of judgement, as Kant seems to suggest? If it is all about subjective judgements, how could this inspire thinkers of politics, who, by very definition of the task in hand, are compelled to think about the universality of political claims? Why, indeed, bother to theorise aesthetics if it is nothing but individual preferences?

The peculiar aspect of Kant's aesthetics is that, rather than establishing rules for distinguishing the beautiful, it establishes judgements of taste as an equally shared capacity in all human beings. It is, in this sense, 'something of an oddity in the history of aesthetics. It does not establish conceptual rules for the beautiful, to the end of constituting a science of the beautiful (that is, aesthetics in the spirit of the eighteenth century)' (Gasché 2003: 3). Kant maintains that we all, by our very nature as human beings, have the ability to make judgements of taste; that is, to judge things as beautiful or sublime. Judgements of taste are not aesthetic because they are about appreciating beautiful objects or events. Indeed, an aesthetic judgement in the Kantian sense does not even refer to any descriptive qualities of the object. All it does is to 'affirm' its beauty, if it is so judged. As Panagia (2006: 70) puts it, in an aesthetic judgement, 'we *affirm* rather than declare an object beautiful and we *presume* that everyone understands such an affirmation'. Judgements of taste are aesthetic because they are about being affected by an object or an event.

In an aesthetic judgement, our relation to the world is one of sensibility rather than one of knowing. We neither identify nor determine anything in the object presented to our senses, but judge it solely in its particularity as it is presented to our senses, without subsuming it under a general rule. This means that an aesthetic judgement is subjective not because it is about individual preferences, but because it is not based on a concept about the object, and, in this sense, it is not dependent on the object. All aesthetic judgements, Kant holds, are singular judgements where we judge the object or event in its singularity.[5] The political implication here is that, rather than silencing the demand of the other to be judged in her singularity, an aesthetic orientation demands that we leave aside given categorisations and classifications, and judge particulars in their singularity – Castella as a judging subject rather than a vulgar industrialist; revolting *banlieue* youth as citizens manifesting their discontent (as, for example, revolting farmers and fishermen are seen) rather than as 'scum' (as one French president put it); *sans papiers* as equals rather than as 'illegal immigrants'.

One of the implications of such an understanding of aesthetic judgement is communicability, which Arendt, in particular, found politically appealing for the creation of common worlds. As Panagia (2006: 72) puts it, aesthetic judgement thus understood 'both presumes and produces a commitment to sociability'. For Kant, judgement is something other than a cognitive truth claim. Aesthetic judgements do not compel agreement in the way demonstrable facts or truth claims do. But they are not merely about subjective preferences either, because in judgements of taste there is a claim on the agreement from others. Kant insists that judgements of taste must 'be able to be universally communicated' (*CJ* §21). As he puts it in §8 of the third Critique,

> there can be . . . no rule in accordance with which someone could be compelled to acknowledge something as beautiful. Whether a garment, a house, a flower is beautiful: no one allows himself to be talked into

his judgement about that by means of any grounds or fundamental principles. One wants to submit the object to his own eyes, just as if his satisfaction depended on sensation; and yet, if one then calls the object beautiful, one believes oneself to have a universal voice, and lays claim to the consent of everyone, whereas any private sensation would be decisive only for him alone and his satisfaction.

Kant is careful to note that the universal voice here is 'only an idea', and that a judgement of taste 'does not itself *postulate* the accord of everyone . . . it only *ascribes* this agreement to everyone' (*CJ* §8). In other words, our aesthetic judgements are not made in a universal voice, and they are not determinative for others. In making such judgements, we merely lay a claim to the agreement of others, which gives our judgements a quality of publicity and communicability that distinguishes them from other forms of judgements that do not necessarily demand a community of judging persons. Arendt (1977: 219) sees here a similarity between aesthetic judgements and political opinions in that they are both persuasive: 'the judging person – as Kant says quite beautifully – can only "woo the consent of everyone else" in the hope of coming to an agreement with him eventually'.[6] What is at stake here is not knowledge or truth, but rather a commitment to communicability that would allow an exchange of opinions and judgements regarding the 'sphere of public life and the common world, and the decision what manner of action is to be taken in it, as well as to how it is to look henceforth, what kind of things are to appear in it' (Arendt 1977: 219–20).

What, then, makes aesthetic judgements universally communicable so that we can lay a claim on the agreement of others? What grants them validity once we have excluded truth and consensus? Kant wrestled with this question in the third Critique, and his answer was that we all share a *sensus communis* that makes such judgements universally communicable and grants them a certain validity. Common sense – *sensus communis* – is not an empirical problem for Kant. It is not a standard, rule or principle to be applied – not, in other words, something that governs judgement. Yet, it is something we appeal to when we make aesthetic judgements so that they become universally communicable rather than remain merely subjective preferences. Common sense, as understood by Kant, is something that we can assume to be shared by all. Or, as Allison (2001: 149) puts it, 'it is a shared capacity to feel what may be universally shareable'.[7]

It is this presupposition of a shared capacity that makes aesthetic judgements universally communicable. If we did not share such a sense or capacity, Kant argues, our judgements 'would have no correspondence with the object: they would all be a merely subjective play of the powers of representation, just as scepticism insists' (*CJ* §21). Thus, the idea of universal communicability based on common sense as shared sense or capacity is what allows our judgements to go beyond a mere subjective play of our mental faculties (Ferrara 2008). This capacity requires, for Kant, that the judging person 'broaden' her way of thinking:

> By '*sensus communis*' . . . must be understood the idea of a communal sense, i.e., a faculty for judging that in its reflection takes account (*a priori*) of everyone else's way of representing in thought, in order as it were to hold its judgement up to human reason as a whole and thereby avoid the illusion which, from subjective private conditions that could easily be held to be objective, would have detrimental influence on the judgement. (*CJ* §40; see also §§20, 21)

The Kantian notion of common sense implies that the judging person put herself 'into the position of everyone else', thus 'abstracting from the limitations that contingently attach to our own judging' (*CJ* §40). Private interests and motivations are left aside when judging aesthetically. It is here that Arendt sees the political import of Kant's notion of *sensus communis*: it 'liberates' our judgements from the confines of our own subjectivity and makes them communicable. This does not imply that the judging person actually communicate with others, but it requires that she 'broaden' her way of thinking and judge, as Arendt puts it, with an 'enlarged mentality'.[8] This enlarged mentality, for Arendt (1992: 73), is

> the condition *sine qua non* of right judgment; one's community sense makes it possible to enlarge one's mentality. Negatively speaking, this means that one is able to abstract from private conditions and circumstances, which, as far as judgment is concerned, limit and inhibit its exercise. Private conditions condition us; imagination and reflection enable us to *liberate* ourselves from them and to attain that relative impartiality that is the specific virtue of judgment. The less idiosyncratic one's taste is, the better it can be communicated; communicability is again the touchstone.

This is one reason why Kant's *Critique of Practical Reason* is not of much help to Arendt, because it is 'based upon the necessity for rational thought to agree with itself' (Arendt 1977: 216). In the *Critique of Judgment*, however, Kant proposed another way of thinking 'for which it would not be enough to be in agreement with one's own self, but which consisted of being able to "think in the place of everybody else"' (Arendt 1977: 217). Arendt thus embraced Kant's aesthetics in her politics for its implications of plurality and communicability, which allowed her to conceive of a political aesthetic that emphasised the creation of common worlds by opening up spaces of relationality. Let us now take a closer look at Arendt's political aesthetic and its Kantian inspirations.

Plurality and Common Worlds

> There cannot be any science of the beautiful and the judgment of taste is not determinable by principles.
>
> (Kant, *Critique of Judgment*, §60)

> What, however, is quite new and even startlingly new in Kant's propositions in the *Critique of Judgement* is that he discovered this phenomenon [judgement] in all its grandeur precisely when he was examining the phenomenon of taste and hence the only kind of judgements which, since they concern merely aesthetic matters, have always been supposed to lie outside the political realm as well as the domain of reason.
>
> (Arendt, *Between Past and Future*, 218)

Kant faced a problem after having finished his first and second critiques: *Critique of Pure Reason*, on the mental abilities of cognition as part of our experience of the world, and *Critique of Practical Reason*, on those of reasoning as they relate to our capacity for moral action. The problem was that these critiques, in dealing with the opposed realms of nature (first Critique) and freedom (second Critique), left the human agent between cognition – governed by the laws of nature – and morality, which implies freedom and free will. In a sense, Kant established, as Arendt (1977: 143) puts it, an 'antinomy between practical freedom and theoretical non-freedom'. We have free will and are free in the moral world, but we are not free in the world of nature, because the natural world and our capacity to know the things in it are governed by the laws of nature and the rules of cognition. Even if we are free as moral agents, we are unable to intervene in the world of objects. Arendt (1977: 143–4) saw here a political problem:

> For the moment we reflect upon an act which was undertaken under the assumption of our being a free agent, it seems to come under the sway of two kinds of causality, of the causality of inner motivation on one hand and of the causal principle which rules the outer world on the other. Kant saved freedom from this twofold assault upon it by distinguishing between a 'pure' or theoretical reason and a 'practical reason' whose centre is free will, whereby it is important to keep in mind that the free-willing agent, who is practically all-important, never appears in the phenomenal world, neither in the outer world of our five senses nor in the field of the inner sense with which I sense myself. This solution . . . does little to eliminate the greatest and most dangerous difficulty, namely, that thought itself, in its theoretical as well as its pre-theoretical form, makes freedom disappear.

If everything were governed by given laws, rules, concepts or standards, new beginnings in the world – the essence of being and action for Arendt, as we will see in the next chapter – would not be possible. As we saw in the previous section, Kant's third Critique offered a notion of aesthetic judgement that provided freedom from such limitations, thus making intervention in the world possible and 'bridging the gap' between his two previous critiques (Hughes 2010). This was something that his *Critique of Practical Reason* – 'what is usually considered to be Kant's political philosophy' (Arendt 1977: 216) – was unable to provide. The third Critique, however, was different in that it made worldly engagement possible. As Arendt puts it:

> The *Critique of Judgment* is the only [one of Kant's] great writings where his point of departure is the World and the senses and capabilities which made men (in the plural) fit to be inhabitants of it. This is perhaps not yet political philosophy, but it certainly is its condition *sine qua non*.[9]

The political lessons Arendt draws from Kant's notion of aesthetic judgement relate first to the lack of standards and rules. Judgements of taste are not governed by such limitations, and we all equally and distinctively share a capacity to make aesthetic judgements. This capacity, for Arendt, suggests that we are capable of going beyond mindlessly applying the rules and blindly following the standards. It is a capacity that keeps open the possibility for the emergence of something new in the midst of ordinary routine and established norms. This may result in a 'loss of standards', but this is not a tragedy unless one assumes that people are 'incapable of judging things per se, that their faculty of judgement is inadequate for making original judgements, and that the most we can demand of it is the correct application of familiar rules derived from already established standards' (Arendt 2005: 104). This is partly why Arendt finds Kant's notion of aesthetic judgement politically pertinent: it presumes a shared capacity that allows for something new to emerge, which, as we will see in the next chapter, resonates strongly with her own emphasis on a shared capacity for action and new beginnings as distinctive features of each human being. Thus, for her, this understanding of aesthetic judgement is 'perhaps the greatest and most original aspect of Kant's political philosophy' (Arendt 1977: 216).

But there is another implication of Kant's notion that Arendt finds politically promising. She sees the faculty of judgement as a political capacity, and judging a political activity, for it suggests a shift from the self towards others. Judgement, in other words, implies plurality, which, for Arendt (1958: 7), is 'specifically *the* condition . . . of all political life'. A fully human life, for her, is possible only through action and speech within the plurality of others in the public realm.

Plurality is the cornerstone of Arendt's political aesthetic. It is, indeed, the very condition of reality in an appearing world. 'For us', she writes, 'appearance – something that is being seen and heard by others as well as by ourselves – constitutes reality'. In other words, it is the 'presence of others who see what we see and hear what we hear [that] assures us of the reality of the world and ourselves' (Arendt 1958: 50). This plurality, as she puts is, is 'the law of the earth':

> Nothing could appear, the word 'appearance' would make no sense, if recipients of appearances did not exist – living creatures able to acknowledge, recognize, and react to – in flight or desire, approval or disapproval, blame or praise – what is not merely there but appears to them and is meant for their perception . . . Nothing and nobody exists in this world whose very being does not presuppose a *spectator*. In other words, nothing that is, insofar as it appears, exists in the singular; everything that is is meant to be perceived by somebody . . . Plurality is the law of the earth. (Arendt 1978/I: 19)

With this presumption of plurality that assures the existence of 'what is', Arendt develops her political aesthetic, first in terms of action, then, later in life, in terms of reflection. There is, however, a tension that runs through Arendt's writings on judgement. In her earlier writings, she focuses on the relationship between judgement and action, where judgement is seen to guide political actors. In her later writings, however, Arendt (1978/I: 96) explores judgement from the viewpoint of the spectator reflecting on the meaning and significance of past events, and argues that 'the spectator, not the actor, holds the clue to the meaning of human affairs' – seemingly almost a reversal of her previous position that seemed to privilege *vita activa* over *vita contemplativa*.[10]

This apparent shift 'from the judgement of the engaged political actor . . . to that of the detached spectator' (Villa 2000: 16) gave rise to a debate about whether Arendt had two different theories of judgement. Passerin d'Entrèves (2000: 246) refers to these as two different 'models', one based on the standpoint of the actor, the other on that of the spectator. In the former, 'judgment is the faculty of political actors acting in the public realm', who are judging to act. In the latter, judgement is the privilege of spectators, who are judging 'to cull meaning from the past'. Whereas in the former judgement is a feature of political life as such in that it guides the actions of political actors in the public realm, in the latter it is a distinct mental activity, a part of 'the life of the mind' – the title of Arendt's three-volume work on 'thinking', 'willing' and 'judging', the last of which she did not live to finish.

In my view, however, Arendt's remarks on the actor and the spectator are best understood as part of her political aesthetic, rather than as two different models or as a valorisation of reflection over action. Arendt is consistent about the hallmark of her political thought – plurality – throughout her work, which is an essential part of her political aesthetic based on disclosure. We act in and make sense of the world of appearances in the plurality of others rather than in isolated contemplation. Whether practical (actor) or contemplative (spectator), Arendt's understanding of judgement requires plurality and disclosure, where actors and spectators are exposed to one another, making every actor a potential spectator as well. This is so because we are capable of stepping into as well as stepping back from action in the public realm. We share a capacity not only to act, but to stop and think as well. 'All thinking demands a *stop*-and-think', Arendt (1978/I: 78) writes, and thinking is key to understanding, which she sees as 'the other side of action':

Even though we have lost yardsticks by which to measure, and rules under which to subsume the particular, a being whose essence is beginning may have enough of origin within himself to understand without preconceived categories and to judge without the set of customary rules which is morality. If the essence of all, and in particular of political, action is to make a new beginning, then understanding becomes the other side of action. (Arendt 1994: 321)[11]

Understanding involves a capacity to step back, to stop and think, which interrupts the numbing effects of being caught up in things. It is this capacity to reflect on and judge actions that allows us to 'eventually come to terms with what irrevocably happened and be reconciled with that unavoidably exists' (Arendt 1994: 322). Thinking is a reflective withdrawal, not an isolation from worldly matters and appearances. This reflective withdrawal is also the interruptive element. Thinking, like action, suggests an interruption in ordinary routine because it requires a 'withdrawal from the course of events' (Buckler 2011: 33). Dark times are around us not only when our capacity of engagement in, but also of withdrawal from, the public realm is compromised; it was precisely the eradication of the capacity for freely acting, thinking and judging that characterised totalitarian regimes for Arendt. Arendt's own reflection about judgement was facilitated by her coverage of the Eichmann trial, and we must remember that she is 'a thinker for whom thoughtlessness accompanied the greatest of modern political disasters' (McClure 1997: 62). It is then politically important to be able to stop and think in order to reflect upon the matters and processes we are caught up with rather than going along with routine. Just like the capacity to act, this is a shared capacity that allows for the interruption of rules and standards to start something new.

I do not, therefore, think that Arendt somehow 'sacrificed' political action in favour of a detached spectatorship; the life of the political actor and the life of the mind are not mutually exclusive.[12] As I suggested above, her distinction between the actor and the spectator is best understood as part of her political aesthetic that emphasises disclosure in a context of plurality, which is a central theme throughout her work. This is what Curtis (1997) refers to as her 'ontology of display', which requires a mutual sensuous provocation between actors and spectators. In a context of plurality, the actions of the actors as well as the responses and opinions of the spectators are important. When the actors expose themselves in public, they become susceptible to and eligible for judgement. They act in the light of public exposure and anticipate judgement that will confer meaning upon their actions. This implies that exposure to judgement is an intrinsic, rather than a contingent, part of action (Buckler 2011). Arendt's political aesthetic demands this plurality and mutual exposure.

It is through this mutual exposure that 'what is' comes into being. This, then, implies that we make sense of the appearing world through encounters, not in isolated reflection. Arendt insists, in Curtis's words (1997: 45), 'that "there is a there there" that we must not submit to but encounter'. Hers is a political aesthetic that implies the creation of common worlds through encounters. This may seem more evident in the case of acting with and in the presence of others, but even judging, as Arendt sees it, is a world-making practice because it demands the presence of others. We have seen above how the notion of judgement Arendt appropriates from Kant's aesthetic theory presumes communicability and sociability. This takes us to the core of Arendt's political aesthetic – plurality – which she saw as '*the* condition of all political life':

> The power of judgement rests on a potential agreement with others, and the thinking process which is active in judging something is not, like the thought process of pure reasoning, a dialogue between me and myself, but finds itself always and primarily, even if I am quite alone in making up my mind, in an anticipated communication with others with whom I know I must finally come to some agreement . . . [Judgement] needs the presence of others 'in whose place' it must think, whose perspectives it must take into consideration . . . As logic, to be sound, depends on the presence of the self, so judgement, to be valid, depends on the presence of others. Hence judgement is endowed with a certain specific validity but is never universally valid. (Arendt 1977: 217)

This is what makes the capacity to judge 'a specifically political ability', for Arendt, because it demands that one see things from the perspective of all others present rather than only from their point of view – with an 'enlarged mentality', as she calls it following Kant. She is thus committed to the idea that aesthetic judgements are universally communicable because we share common sense. If we did not have such a presupposition, we would lose all possibility for the creation of common worlds, which is central to her political aesthetic. The creation of common worlds, through acting or judging, demands an engagement with manifold others without necessarily postulating unity, agreement or consensus. Common sense, writes Arendt (1977: 218), 'discloses to us the nature of the world insofar as it is a common world . . . Judging is one, if not the most, important activity in which this sharing-the-world-with-others comes to pass'.[13]

For Arendt (1992: 70), this notion of common sense indicates 'an extra sense – like an extra mental capacity . . . – that fits us into a community'. She argues that *sensus communis* for Kant is community sense (unlike *sensus privatus*), and it is this 'communal' aspect that gives judgements validity: 'This *sensus communis* is what judgment appeals to in everyone, and it is this possible appeal that gives judgements their special validity' (Arendt 1992: 72). Arendt sees in Kant an understanding of judgement that relies neither on truth nor on consensus. This resonates well with her understanding of politics, which, she argues, cannot be conceived around truth claims, because truth compels assent.[14] We can at best 'woo' or 'court' the agreement of others, but our judgements do not compel agreement. As she puts it,

> one can never compel anyone to agree with one's judgments – 'This is beautiful' or 'This is wrong' . . . one can only 'woo' or 'court' the agreement of everyone else. And in this persuasive activity one actually appeals to the 'community sense'. In other words, when one judges, one judges as a member of a community. (Arendt 1992: 72)

This raises a question as to whether common sense is empirical (a product of actual communities) or transcendental (a given condition of judgement), as Kant seems to suggest. Here Beiner and Nedelsky (2001) spot a difference between Arendt and Kant. What makes judgements possible and universally communicable is 'common sense' for both, but they conceive its source differently. For Kant, common sense is part of our faculties. For Arendt (1977: 217), however,

> judgment is endowed with a certain specific validity but is never universally valid. Its claims to validity can never extend further than the others in whose place the judging person has put himself for his considerations. Judgment, Kant says, is valid 'for every single judging person', but the emphasis in the sentence is on 'judging'; it is not valid for those who do not judge or for those who are not members of the public realm where the objects of judgment appear.

Arendt thus limits the validity of judgement to a shared public domain defined by the practice of judging, or, as Beiner and Nedelsky (2001: p. xi) put it, to a 'community of judging subjects'. So, while common sense for Kant is 'natural', for Arendt it seems more of a historical or empirical problem based in actual community rather than a given capacity. Arendt's distinctive contribution here, they argue, is 'basing judgement in actual community'. Beiner (1992) elsewhere raises this issue, arguing for a grounding of the practice of judging in concrete community. For Villa (2001: 301), however, such communitarian renderings 'radically devalue the aesthetic dimension of Arendt's theory of judgement'. In trying to 'correct' Arendt's notion of judgement by situating it in actual community, such renderings seem to neglect why Arendt was attracted to Kant's aesthetics in the first place. What is significant in Kant's idea of aesthetic judgement is that the individual is not subsumed under community, and in following him what Arendt has in mind is a notion of 'worldliness' that is 'not reducible to the "situatedness" promoted by the communitarians' (Villa 2001: 302). As Arendt (1977: 219) herself puts it:

> The activity of taste decides how this world, independent of its utility and our vital interests in it, is to look and sound, what men will see and what they will hear in it. Taste judges the world in its appearance and in its worldliness; its interest in the world is purely 'disinterested', and that means that neither the life interests of the individual nor the moral interests of the self are involved here. For judgements of taste, the world is the primary thing, not man, neither man's life nor his self.

This tension is not entirely resolved by Arendt, but, given her broader political project, communitarian renderings of her work seem to me misleading. The creation of common worlds is key to Arendt's politics, but her notion of common world does not imply a single vision of the world to which everyone subscribes. Such an agreed upon vision is the end, rather than the condition, of the common world. 'The end of the common world has come', she writes, 'when it is seen only under one aspect and is permitted to present itself in only one perspective (Arendt 1958: 58). Unlike Nancy, whom I will turn to in the next section, Arendt does not conceive the common world as an ontological condition of existence. For her, the common world is something to be attained, and is, therefore, a 'political achievement' (Zerilli 2012: 23) rather than an ontological given.[15]

Therefore, the creation of common worlds in the Arendtian sense does not require a community unified around a collective identity or ideal, but depends, as we have seen above, on the idea of communicability. The notion of judgement Arendt appropriates from Kant does not presume the stability of a given communitarian grounding or horizon. It is based on the possibility of opening up new spaces as shared domains of experience where actors disclose themselves and are exposed to one another. This is what she calls, as we will see in the next chapter, 'spaces of appearance', which are not already given domains of experience, but spaces opened up by distinctive gatherings of actors. It is through such episodic and collective spatialisations that actors and spectators relate to one another and experience their world as common. As we will see in the next section, the constitution of the common through spatialisation is a main theme in Nancy as well, but his conceptualisation extends this idea to everything that exists. He focuses on Kant's notion of 'presentation' that allows engagement with the world possible in freedom from conceptual determination.

The One and the Other

> We share what divides us: the freedom of an incalculable and improbable *coming* to presence of being, which only brings us into presence as the *ones* of the *others*.
>
> (Nancy, *The Experience of Freedom*, 95)

What Nancy finds appealing in Kant's third Critique is the notion of 'presentation'. However, some of the key elements of Arendt's political aesthetic – plurality, mutual exposure, creation of worlds – are central features of his as well. Nancy's political aesthetic emphasises the creation and disclosure of a 'common' world in freedom. That this world is created and disclosed in freedom means that it does not bear an originary or given meaning. Nancy's politics thus demands an engagement with the world in freedom, making sense of it without pre-given determinations. Kant's notion of aesthetic judgement as judgement without criteria suggests a way of engaging with the world in this way, apprehending it in the absence of rules and standards, free from pre-given conceptual determinations. It thus allows a way of engaging with the world that is neither epistemically nor morally determined (Hughes 2010), signalling a certain freedom in the creation of a world and in making sense of it.

'Sense' is one of Nancy's concepts to think existence in the world. He uses it to suggest not only meaning and signification, but also sensation and movement towards something (as implied in the various meanings of the French *sens*). The possibility of apprehending and making sense of the world depends on a movement towards the other with which a being is in common existence. Therefore, when Nancy (1997: 54) talks about 'the sense of the world', he is not referring to the world 'as a factual given on which one would come to confer a sense'. World 'means at least *being-to* or *being-toward* [être-à]; it means rapport, relation, address, sending, donation, presentation *to* – if only of entities or existents to each other'. This implies that world itself is 'structured as *sense*, and reciprocally, *sense* is structured as *world*' (Nancy 1997: 8).

Sense and world are therefore co-constitutive. Since sense is not given, but made in the plurality of encounters, this implies that a world is not a given factual and objective entity. The world suggests, as sense does, relation, exposure and 'spaciosity', a term Nancy uses to refer to spatial taking form in the world and of the world, as we will see in more detail in Chapter 4. 'A world', Nancy (2000a: 185) writes, 'is a multiplicity of worlds; the world is a multiplicity of worlds, and its unity is the mutual sharing and exposition of all its worlds – within this world'. 'World' thus becomes part of Nancy's ontology of coexistence, according to which whatever exists coexists, and this implies 'the sharing of the world'. A world, then, is intrinsic to existence as coexistence. It is 'not something external to existence; it is not an extrinsic addition to other existences; the world is the coexistence that puts these existences together' (Nancy 2000a: 29). It is in and through worlds that beings take spatial form, share space, relate to one another, disclose themselves and get exposed to others. For all these to take place, a world is necessary, not as external to this taking place, but as an integral part of it. A world, to put it differently, is not a container where all merely appears. 'Nothing happens in a world that would be a container,' as Nancy (2013: 113) puts it. A world is the space of taking place: 'What takes place takes place in a world and by way of that world. A world is the common place of a totality of places: of presences and dispositions for possible events' (Nancy 2007: 42).

But what form does a world take? What makes apprehension of and engagement with a world possible? This is where the Kantian notion of presentation informs Nancy's conceptualisation. In Section VIII of his introduction to the third Critique, Kant defines the role of presentation as follows: 'If the concept of an object is given, then the business of the power of judgement in using it for cognition consists in presentation (*exhibitio*), i.e., in placing a corresponding intuition beside the concept.' Presentation makes concepts intuitable, thus mediating between sensibility and understanding. For Kant, intuitions (sensibility) and concepts (understanding) depend on each other for knowledge. We produce 'instances' of concepts in intuition, which take the form of time and space. In other words, when we 'present' a concept, this means that we have associated it with a distinctive spatial or temporal form in intuition (Henrich 1992). There is, therefore, an already given concept that corresponds to what we perceive.

However, as we have seen, aesthetic judgements are free from conceptual determination. The specificity of an aesthetic judgement is precisely that what is presented to our senses is not governed by an already given concept. What happens when we are dealing with phenomena that are given in experience, but have no conceptual determination? This is where presentation comes into play so that we can give form to the manifold of intuition that we encounter. Without presentation, it would not be possible to represent anything; we would have pure multiplicity. As Gasché (2003: 118) puts it, 'without a presentation, no representation of a "something" in general would be possible'. Presentation, therefore, is an essential component of our experience of the empirical world, allowing us to give form to what we perceive even if we do not possess a concept to determine it – allowing us, in other words, to apprehend it in its and our freedom.

Alison Ross (2007) was the first to explore in detail this aspect of Nancy's work. She argues that, with the notion of presentation, Kant defines a mode of relation to the world to reconcile freedom with the constraints of materiality. This aesthetic mode of relation to the world allows us 'to render in aesthetic or sensible forms what would otherwise be impotent, errant ideas' (Ross 2007: 2). It is presentation that makes our engagement with the world possible, allowing us to engage with the world and make sense of it in freedom from conceptual determination, which is also where, as we have seen, Arendt saw the political appeal of the third Critique. As Gasché (2003: 98–9) explains:

If presentation gains a conspicuous role in the Third Critique, this is not because reflective aesthetic judgment is aesthetic in the sense that it would deal with the beautiful in art and artistic representation ... Rather, presentation is important because aesthetic reflective judgments originate when one is faced with a manifold of intuition that precludes determinate concepts.

This is also what Nancy finds appealing in the third Critique. Ross (2007: 134) argues that presentation as sense or meaning is 'the central topic in Nancy's thought'. Sense depends on aesthetic forms and requires engagement with the world, and the perspective Ross opens shows the importance of appearance, sense and worldlihood for Nancy. As we will see in more detail in Chapter 4, Nancy's ontology depends on an understanding of existence as coexistence. This suggests a spatial taking form in the world and of the world where spacing is not just exteriority or an order of relations, but the very condition of existence, freedom and sense.

Sense is never given or complete for Nancy. It is the worldly presence of being, existence in common spaces of sharing. Just as beings are thrown into plurality, they are thrown into sense. Sense comes to presence in the spacing of this multiplicity of singularities. Nancy emphasises at once plurality and singularity, which demands the possibility of the apprehension of each being in their freedom, a possibility Kant's notion of aesthetic judgement provides. Sense, then, is contingent on relations in a context of plurality. It is not represented as truth (as in, for example, figures or myths of community, nation, and so on), but presented in sensible forms. This is the aesthetic and spatial dimension of Nancy's ontology; namely, emergence of sense from what is available to the senses.

Presentation is 'the spacing of sense' (Nancy 2003: 24). Finding worldly meaning requires spacing and aesthetic forms that are presented in their freedom, without conceptual determination. Presentation makes this possible because it allows for the formation of forms in their freedom. This has political implications. As we will see in Chapter 4, Nancy's understanding of politics involves doing away with 'common sense' in order to open up the possibility for the multiplicity of 'sense in-common'. This requires the possibility of interrupting habitual or routinised ways of perceiving the world and modes of relating to it while allowing for the capacity to exhibit and apprehend aesthetic forms.[16] Presentation makes world disclosure and engagement with the world possible. Indeed, without presentation, it would not be possible to appear and be apprehended as singularities. As Nancy (2007: 60) puts it, 'what is necessary is a world that would only be the world of singularities, without their plurality constructed as a unitotality'. As we will see in the following section, Rancière also posits the disruption of common ways of perceiving the world and making sense of it – 'distribution of the sensible', in his terminology – as a defining feature of politics, but his adoption of Kant's aesthetics differs from both Arendt's and Nancy's.

Radical Equality

In an essay entitled 'The Skeptic', David Hume (2008: 98) wrote:

> There is something approaching to principles in mental taste; and critics can reason and dispute more plausibly than cooks or perfumers. We may observe, however, that this uniformity among human kind hinders not, but that there is a considerable diversity in the sentiments of beauty and worth, and that education, custom, prejudice, caprice, and humour, frequently vary our taste of this kind.

Kant's response was the following:

> Thus although critics, as Hume says, can reason more plausibly than cooks, they still suffer the same fate as them. They cannot expect a *determining ground* for their judgement from proofs, but only from the reflection of the subject on his own state (of pleasure or displeasure), *rejecting all precepts and rules.* (CJ §34; emphasis added)

There, then, we have it: anyone – be it a cook or a critic, an actor or a factory-owner – has the capacity to make aesthetic judgements for such judgements are not determined by knowledge, standards or rules. Kant thus refuses to submit the capacity for aesthetic judgement under established principles or the qualities of the person making the judgement. The radical implication is that anyone is capable of aesthetic judgements; one does not need to know the rules (there are none), have certain qualifications or mental capacities to be able to make judgements of taste. Kant's aesthetics thus carries with it a radically egalitarian politics, as it not only declines to attribute norms, standards or rules to aesthetic judgement – thereby removing possible sources of privilege and authority – but also implies the possibility of disrupting consolidated subject positions, indeed of any ground for privilege and hierarchy.

This is not an 'aesthetic illusion' (Eagleton 1990), but an aesthetic suspension: of knowledge, skills, legitimacy and established distribution of roles and aptitudes. In Kant's notion of aesthetic judgement, there is a moment of interruption when the subject's interests, cognitive determination, desires and ambitions are suspended. For Hughes (2010), this suspension of our dominant inclinations opens up a different kind of attention and implies an alternative way of relating to the world, suggesting thus a politics. Panagia (2009) draws the political implications of this interruption by arguing that Kant's third Critique provides a theory of decentred subject and a critique of privilege, and refers to this as Kant's 'radical democratic project'. There is indeed something radically egalitarian in Kant's conception of aesthetic judgement. Rancière turns Kant's postulate of a universally shared capacity for aesthetic judgement into a political principle of axiomatic equality – the equality of anyone with anyone. This 'challenge of equality' (Thomson 2011: 200) demands that equality be affirmed and actualised in time and space, which implies a disruption of habitual ways of perceiving the world and making sense of it.[17] But this is not the only Kantian element that informs Rancière. In his conceptualisation of politics, Rancière establishes a relationship between equality, aesthetics and dissensus based on an unorthodox interpretation of Kant's first and third Critiques.[18] In addition to axiomatic equality, then, there are two more Kantian legacies in Rancière's political thought: aesthetics, as consolidated orders of time and space, and dissensus, as occasioned by aesthetic experience.[19]

Aesthetics, for Rancière, is at the core of politics, but this has nothing to do with Walter Benjamin's notion of 'aestheticisation of politics' associated with the age of masses. 'This aesthetics', he writes, 'should not be understood as the perverse commandeering of politics by a will to art, by a consideration of the people qua work of art' (Rancière 2004a: 13). Indeed, he even argues that 'there never has been any "aestheticization" of politics in the modern age because politics is aesthetic in principle' (Rancière 1999: 58). Politics, for Rancière, is a polemical redistribution of spaces and times, objects and subjects, meanings and visibilities, and it is in this sense that it can be thought of as an 'aesthetic activity' (Rancière 2009a: 32). This suggests that politics is an aesthetic as well as a spatial affair, for it is about the distribution of what is presented to sense experience.

This aesthetic and spatial aspect of Rancière's political thought has its sources in his earlier, more 'historical' work; notably, *The Nights of Labour*, *The Philosopher and His Poor* and *The Ignorant Schoolmaster* (although his conceptual interest in 'space' pre-dates these, as we shall see in Chapter 5). As he puts it himself (Rancière 2005), the aesthetic dimension of politics has been his basic concern throughout his research. When considering the aesthetic dimension of politics, Rancière (2005: 13) admittedly uses the term 'aesthetic' in a sense 'close to the Kantian idea of "a priori forms of sensibility": it is not a matter of art and taste; it is, first of all, a matter of time and space'.[20] Although not conceptually organised around aesthetics, *The Nights of Labour* (1989) was a prime example of this, where Rancière provided an account of the ordering of the time and space of workers. The division they had to abide by – work and rest – prevented them from doing anything other than what this partitioning imposed. At night, the worker had to sleep rather than think or write or discuss so that she would be ready for work the next morning. Emancipation implied undoing this order. This is a common thread in Rancière's work: that systems of domination impose or consolidate temporal and spatial orders that 'wrong' equality, and politics is about disrupting them. This is the relationship that he establishes between equality, aesthetics and dissensus.

This aesthetic dimension is the second Kantian legacy in Rancière's politics. But this is the aesthetic of Kant's first Critique, *Critique of Pure Reason*, rather than the aesthetics of his third Critique. Kant's transcendental philosophy is concerned with the *a priori* conditions that make our experience of the world possible, and the focus of his first Critique is on the mental abilities of cognition as part of our experience of the world. Space and time, for Kant, are part of a 'transcendental aesthetic'; they are not derived from experience, but are given to us as *a priori* forms of sensibility to provide form to our experience of the world. Thus, although space and time make our experience of the world possible, they do not rely on experience; they merely give form to our awareness of things we encounter in the empirical world. This brings us back to the question that was raised in the introduction: what, then, gives space form? If spatial form is already given, how can a link between space and politics be established?

Rancière does not follow Kant to the letter; his is an interpretation rather than an application of the Kantian idea of time and space as *a priori* forms of sensibility. He specifies that he 'does not deal with time and space as forms of presentation of the objects of our knowledge', which would be the strict Kantian version. For him, they are 'forms of configuration of our "place" in society, forms of distribution of the common and the private, and of assignation to everybody of his or her own part' (Rancière 2005: 13). If Kant dealt with the aesthetic in terms of *a priori* forms that order what presents itself to sense experience, Rancière deals with it as what he calls a 'distribution of the sensible' (*le partage du sensible*), evoking at once the first Critique's concern with the form of what is presented to the senses, and the third Critique's concern with aesthetics as a way of engaging with the world. Or, to put it in the language I have been using, aesthetics is linked to politics as a form of perceiving the world and a mode of relating to it.

The word *partage* in 'partage du sensible' is oxymoronic as it means both 'partition' and 'sharing'. Rancière uses it to refer to what is put in common and shared in the community (*à partager*), as well as to what is separated (*partagé*). There is, however, another meaning of the word: as used in the phrase *en partage*, it refers to an inheritance, an endowment (usually positive, such as talent). So another connotation of 'le partage du sensible' would be to be given (or to have inherited) certain ways of perceiving and making sense of things – habitual, routinised or normalised ways of apprehending the world, the disruption of which, in the name of equality, is the political moment for Rancière. Therefore, Kant's notion of *a priori* forms is both altered and expanded by Rancière. Forms are no longer in the mind (where Kant had them), but in particular historical and geographical contexts. The distribution of the sensible is a contingent ordering of forms that structure common experience, marked by tension and conflict. 'A distribution of the sensible', writes Rancière (2009b: 158), 'is always a state of forces [*état des forces*]'. He is concerned with such orderings, because it is through the consolidation of spatial and temporal orders that the principle of equality is violated.

We have now dealt with the first two of what I call the three Kantian legacies in Rancière's political thought: axiomatic equality and aesthetics. In order to get a sense of the third legacy, dissensus, it will be necessary to revisit Kant's third Critique, and pay attention to the way he conceived of the workings of our faculties in the moment of aesthetic judgement. According to Kant, we have different cognitive faculties that work together. The understanding is the cognitive faculty that provides us the concepts. The imagination 'represents', as it were, the senses. Its role is to hold together under a form what is received by our senses, which then is subsumed under concepts provided by the understanding. There is, therefore, a hierarchical relationship between the understanding and the imagination, where the latter operates under the rules provided by the former to synthesise the manifold of sensory data presented to our senses. What this means is that 'in its ordinary employment, the imagination is not free at all. It operates under the strict rules of the understanding [which provides the concepts]' (Gasché 2003: 149).

If this were always the case, however, aesthetic judgement would not be possible, because, as we have seen, it is based on apprehension in the absence of any determining concepts. Aesthetic judgements demand, in other words, freedom of the imagination from any conceptual determination. So something different happens with aesthetic judgements; the imagination and the understanding enter into a non-hierarchical relationship. They are now in a relation of 'free play', as Kant calls it, where no rule or concept governs (*CJ* §9). This collapse of hierarchy and lack of conceptual determination signals a freedom: there is a moment of freedom in the way I relate to the world, where I can judge an object or event in its particularity – in its, and my, freedom.

Kant thus freed aesthetic experience by disrupting the hierarchical relationship between the intellectual and sensory faculties. However, as Rancière (2009a) observes, the political implications of this de-hierarchisation were not explicitly articulated by Kant, but by Schiller, who followed Kant to define an 'aesthetic state'. Schiller's political genius, according to Rancière, was defining the aesthetic state as 'a sphere of sensory equality where the supremacy of active understanding over passive sensibility was no longer valid'. This implied an egalitarian politics by de-privileging aesthetic experience and thus disrupting the established hierarchy between classes: the 'power of the high classes was supposed to be the power of activity over passivity, of understanding over sensation, of the educated senses over the raw senses' (Rancière 2009a: 37). As Schiller himself wrote in his twenty-seventh letter:

> Everything in the aesthetic State, even the subservient tool, is a free citizen having equal rights with the noblest; and the intellect, which forcibly

moulds the passive multitude to its designs, must here ask for its assent. Here, then, in the realm of aesthetic appearance, is fulfilled the ideal of equality.

Schiller is clearly following Kant's de-hierarchisation of the relationship between the intellectual and sensory faculties. At the moment of aesthetic judgement, what is presented to our senses is not subsumed under a concept; our intellectual and sensory faculties – the understanding and the imagination – are now in free play. What Schiller proposes in his aesthetic state is a form of freedom and equality that has its source in the shared capacity to make aesthetic judgements. Aesthetic judgement is egalitarian for Schiller, for it relates members of society through their common capacity rather than separating them by providing grounds for privilege and hierarchy:

> All other forms of communication divide society, because they relate exclusively either to the private sensibility or to the private skilfulness of its individual members, that is, to what distinguishes between one man and another; only the communication of the Beautiful unites society, because it relates to what is common to them all. (Schiller 2004 [1795]: twenty-seventh letter)

Therefore, aesthetic experience implies the disruption of hierarchical and determinative relations – a sort of aesthetic negation, formulated by Kant, reinterpreted in political terms by Schiller, and adopted by Rancière. This 'Kantian aesthetic negation' suggests a suspension of established rules and power relations that 'usually structure the experience of the knowing, acting and desiring subject' (Rancière 2009c: 97). Thus, aesthetic experience not only 'implies a certain disconnection from the habitual conditions of sensible experience' (Rancière 2006: 1), but also suggests a dissensus, understood here as 'the rupture of a certain agreement between thought and the sensible' that follows from the de-hierarchisation of faculties (Rancière 2009c: 98). This is the third Kantian legacy in Rancière's politics:

> The essence of politics is . . . dissensus. But dissensus is not the opposition of interests or opinions. It is the production, within a determined, sensible world, of a given that is heterogeneous to it. This production defines, in a specific sense, an aesthetic of politics that has nothing to do with the aesthetization of forms of power or the manifestations of collectivity. Politics is aesthetic in that it makes visible what had been excluded from

a perceptual field, and in that it makes audible what used to be inaudible. It inscribes one perceptual world within another. (Rancière 2004b: 226)

Rancière's politics involves disruption of 'common sense', understood as habitual or routinised ways of perceiving and making sense of the world. He starts with a premise – axiomatic equality – but locates moments of its negation or verification in historical contexts. The distribution of the sensible is an empirical problem for Rancière, and it is in these contingent aesthetic orders that his axiomatic equality is 'wronged' by consolidated orders or verified by subjects staging dissensus, altering forms of perceiving the world and modes of relating to it. Rancière thus joins Arendt and Nancy in suggesting a political relation to the world that is not one of knowing, but one of aesthetics. Such an orientation makes possible an understanding of politics as the disruption of normalised coordinates of sensory experience and habitual practices of sense-making, allowing Castella and the cook to undermine grounds of privilege by affirming their capacity, verifying the equality of anyone with anyone.

As this account suggests, perception by the senses – *aisthesis* – is central to the political aesthetic of Arendt, Nancy and Rancière. Their politics requires aesthetic forms and domains of relationality, and in the following three chapters I will show how space performs this function. I will argue that each of them, in their different ways, gives space a fundamental role for the constitution of common worlds of sensory experience, relational domains of experience, and political subjectivities.

Chapter 3
Politics for Beginners

Sans papiers as Beginners

In the centre of Paris, there is a public square called *Place du Châtelet*. Below is the largest underground station of the whole regional network, above are crowds of passers-by and tourists. On Saturday afternoons, there also used to be a gathering of foreigners whose purposes were anything but touristic. These were unregistered immigrants, from a number of countries, demonstrating as part of a larger movement known as the movement of *sans papiers* (literally, 'without papers', meaning they have no official documents allowing or recognising their presence in France). Officially, these people demonstrating at the heart of the French capital did not exist. Yet there they were, chanting and demonstrating, demanding political rights in a country that neither wanted nor allowed them to be there. What is the political significance of exposing themselves to others – to fellow *sans papiers*, allies and opponents, passers-by, the police – and making themselves spatially manifest?

Although the mobilisation of *sans papiers* in France has a longer history going back to the 1970s (Siméant 1998; Cissé 1999), it was the occupation of the Saint-Ambroise church in Paris in 1996 that brought the issue to the attention of a broader public. The occupation took place in a context of increased mobilisation by anti-racist associations in the mid-1990s in response to the increasingly restrictive and repressive measures against immigrants, marked by the passing of the second 'Pasqua law' in 1993.[1] The undocumented immigrants were particularly hard hit by this law, which not only made their 'regularisation' harder and their expulsion easier, but also deprived them of basic social protection, thus leaving them in an extremely precarious situation. As Cissé (1999) explains,[2] many undocumented immigrants initially enter France through regular channels, work, pay taxes and make their social-security contributions, but find themselves 'without papers' when their request for the renewal of their residency permit is refused. What the 1993 Pasqua law did was to make social protection dependent on the 'regularity' of stay; even those who paid their taxes and social-security contributions for years were thus deprived of social protection once they had lost their papers. The occupation of Saint-Ambroise 'gave birth', as Panagia (2006: 120) argues, 'to a new genre of political subjectivity throughout Europe: the *sans papiers*'. The actions of the *sans papiers*, their public exposure and performance, constituted them as political subjects and put them in a position to make political claims.

In *The Origins of Totalitarianism*, Arendt discusses 'rightlessness' and the 'perplexities' of human rights. The first loss of the rightless is the loss of home, which means 'the loss of the entire social texture into which they were born and in which they established for themselves a distinct place in the world' (Arendt 1968: 293). This has important political implications, as Arendt goes on to explain, because being deprived of rights is 'first and foremost being deprived of a place in the world that makes our opinions significant and actions efficient'. The rightless are deprived of the right to action, and thus of a place in the world where 'one is judged by one's actions and opinions' (Arendt 1968: 296–7). Rightlessness means deprivation from politics because it means deprivation from appearance – action and speech in the public realm – which is a core element in Arendt's understanding of politics. How then do we account for the political actions of the *sans papiers* in a context where their presence is officially denied? Or, as Schaap (2011: 33) puts it, 'if statelessness corresponds not only to a situation of rightlessness but also to a life deprived of public appearance, how could those excluded from politics publicly claim the right to have rights, the right to politics?'[3]

The answer, I wish to suggest in this chapter, is that political action inaugurates space. Arendt's remarks above suggest that the challenge is to constitute a space where actions and opinions could be made public. My aim here is to explore this inaugural aspect of Arendt's understanding of politics by following a central theme in her thought: beginning. If, as Arendt argues, all humans are beginners by virtue of birth and have the capacity for new beginnings in the world – a 'second birth', in her words – then there must be some way of restoring an individual's political relation to the world were it ever impaired. Space performs this function by providing a common domain of experience for individuals and putting them in relation to one another. The *sans papiers* might have been deprived of politics following a loss of a place in the world, in Arendtian terms. But they are beginners nonetheless: they constitute themselves as political subjects in and through space, not merely acting in a given space, but making space through their actions. Their actions are inaugurative and disruptive, nothing short of a miracle that allows them to insert themselves into the world 'like a second birth' (Arendt 1958: 176).

I start with miracles in the next section, and introduce natality and the miracle of beginnings as central themes in Arendt's political thought. Space, I argue, accounts for natality as a second birth through which actors insert themselves into the world, which may appear miraculous within the given order of things. In the following two sections, I show how spatialisation enables a political relation to the world and others for Arendt, but also submit that she uses contradictory spatial imaginaries in her conceptualisation of political action. Some of these suggest an absolute spatial compartmentalisation, for which she has been criticised. In the final section, I acknowledge this tension in Arendt's political thought, but argue that there is sufficient evidence in her writings to suggest a relational approach rather than an absolute compartmentalisation of active life into separate domains. Spatialisation allows Arendt to account for the specificity of politics by evoking a distinctive – yet not necessarily absolute – domain that enables actors to be exposed to one another and experience their world as common. Space as a form of appearance and a mode of actuality defines a tangible relation to the world, which is at the heart of Arendt's understanding of political action.

The Miracles of Arendt

I feel so free – things can't stay the same after this.
(Ahmed Ashraf, Tahrir Square, Cairo[4])

The miracle of freedom is inherent in this ability to make a beginning, which itself is inherent in the fact that every human being, simply by being born into a world that was there before him and will be there after him, is himself a new beginning.
(Arendt, *The Promise of Politics*, 113)

Arendt is a theorist of beginnings. Since each individual is a beginning in the world herself, then she can begin something new – at once a beginning and a beginner. This is the human condition of natality for Arendt, which refers not merely to the emergence of life in the world but also to a capacity for new beginnings. This is a capacity to introduce something new into the world, something unexpected and unpredictable so that the world is constantly renewed. What makes new beginnings in the world possible, what allows 'the actualisation of the human condition of natality' (Arendt 1958: 178), is action. As Arendt (1958: 9) puts it, 'the new beginning inherent in birth can make itself felt in the world only because the newcomer possesses the capacity of beginning something anew, that is, of acting'. In contrast to Heidegger's emphasis on human mortality, Arendt focuses on natality to emphasise action as a shared human capacity so that a new beginning, a 'second birth' in the world, is always possible:

> If left to themselves, human affairs can only follow the law of mortality
> . . . It is the faculty of action that interferes with this law because it
> interrupts the inexorable automatic course of daily life . . . The life span
> of man running toward death would inevitably carry everything human
> to ruin and destruction if it were not for the faculty of interrupting it and
> beginning something new, a faculty which is inherent in action like an
> ever-present reminder that men, though they must die, are not born in
> order to die but in order to begin . . . Action is, in fact, the one miracle-
> working faculty of man. (Arendt 1958: 246)

This is the miracle of Arendt. Even in the most discouraging of situations, this 'faculty of freedom', this 'sheer capacity to begin', remains 'intact', but it needs to manifest itself as a 'worldly, tangible reality'[5] to become political. Freedom 'develops fully only when action has created its own worldly space' where it can appear. Arendt's miracle refers to the capacity of individuals to 'establish a reality of their own' – their world – because they are gifted with freedom and action, which always suggests the possibility of new beginnings (Arendt 1977: 167, 169). Natality and the miracle of beginning, then, are central themes in Arendt's conceptualisation of action and politics. 'Since action is the political activity par excellence,' she writes, 'natality, and not mortality, may be the central category of political, as distinguished from metaphysical, thought' (Arendt 1958: 9). Action gives freedom a worldly, tangible quality and allows actors to insert themselves in the world. 'Men *are* free', Arendt (1977: 151) writes, 'as long as they act, neither before nor after; for to *be* free and to act are the same'. This is not, however, the kind of freedom enjoyed individually, such as the liberal notion of the individual enjoying, say, freedom of choice among alternatives. Freedom for Arendt is an activity that consists in acting in the presence of others, in human plurality. Without it, 'political life as such would be meaningless. The *raison d'être* of politics is freedom, and its field of experience is action' (Arendt 1977: 145).

But action alone will not suffice for freedom to become a worldly, tangible reality in the Arendtian sense. Two more conditions are necessary: plurality and spatialisation. It is only in the presence of others and through the creation of a 'space of appearance' that actors insert themselves into the world, which, in the words of Arendt (1958: 176), is 'like a second birth'. As we saw in Chapter 2, plurality is central to Arendt's political aesthetic. Our sense of reality in a world of appearances depends on plurality rather than on isolated contemplation. It is plurality that allows the creation of common worlds, because it allows a variety of perspectives rather than a single vision, which, for Arendt, brings about the end of the common world. Plurality, as she puts it in the opening pages of *The Human Condition*, 'is the condition of human action' (Arendt 1958: 8).

Action is one of the three elements of what Taminiaux (1997) calls Arendt's 'phenomenology of active life'. Labour and work, the other two elements, sustain organic life and provide a world of artefacts (Arendt 1958). Labour allows survival in the biological sense ('The human condition of labour is life itself'), and work provides for the durable and relatively stable world in which individuals act ('The human condition of work is worldliness' (Arendt 1958: 7)). Neither of these requires the sense of publicness that Arendt associates with action, which relies on human plurality for the sharing of words and deeds in a common world. For Arendt, a fully human life is only possible through action and speech in the public realm within the plurality of others. 'Action', she writes, 'corresponds to the human condition of plurality', and 'this plurality is specifically *the* condition . . . of all political life' (Arendt 1958: 7).

Arendtian plurality suggests a relation rather than a multiplication in numbers, as it is not about the number of individuals, but about their distinctiveness. It is the condition of human action because, Arendt (1958: 8) explains, 'we are all the same, that is, human, in such a way that nobody is ever the same as anyone else who ever lived, lives, or will live'. Therefore, two features of human plurality are equality and distinction. 'Human plurality', writes Arendt (1958: 176), 'is the paradoxical plurality of unique beings', and the 'unique distinctness' of each individual is revealed through speech and action in the public realm. The miracle of action interrupts the routine of necessity and consumption, allowing individuals to disclose their distinctiveness – 'who' they are. Arendt distinguishes 'who' someone is from 'what' they are. The former denotes the specific uniqueness of each individual, whereas the latter refers to the predicative qualities that are used to describe and categorise them. Who someone is is disclosed only in action and speech in the public realm, in the plurality of others. This public disclosure of who someone is leads Honig (1995: 3) to argue that Arendt offers significant resources to those who are critical of identity-based politics as 'she theorizes a democratic politics built not on already existing identities or shared experiences but on contingent sites of principled coalescence and shared practices of citizenship'. The promise and significance of political action does not derive from the identity of the actor – what she is – before she steps into action, but from and through her actions with others.

The Arendtian strand of political thought, Marchart (2007) argues, stresses the associative moment of political action because she emphasises 'acting in concert' and 'acting together'.[6] Her understanding of plurality seems to support this qualification, but, as we have seen, this plurality is not merely meant to imply the coming-together of individuals as a collective. Arendt's definition of political action as acting together does not necessarily imply that she is advocating a solidaristic model of political action, not simply because she was highly sceptical of such models, but also because this would neglect her notion of worldliness as central to political life (Villa 2001). Seen as part of her phenomenology of active life, Arendt's notion of plurality implies a political relation and a world-building practice, which is also essential for the actors to disclose their distinctiveness. Even though the contingent sites of political action may arise from shared experience,[7] in each instance a political relationship that did not exist before and a new common world are established. Furthermore, each instance is individuating for the actors themselves, because they disclose and discover who they are by acting in the presence of others. This is not, however, an individualistic or subject-centred account, since Arendt's emphasis is on acting in concert, which has nothing to do with the given attributes of the actor. The actor is constituted in the act, neither prior to nor apart from it, and in the plurality of others rather than in isolation. As Honig (1993: 79–80) puts it:

> Prior to or apart from action, the self is fragmented, discontinuous, indistinct, and most certainly uninteresting. A life-sustaining, psychologically determined, trivial, and imitable biological creature in the private realm, this self attains identity – becomes a 'who' – by acting in the public realm in concert with others. In so doing, it forsakes 'what' it is, the roles and features that define (and even determine) it in the private realm.

Political action in the presence of others is at the origin of Arendt's political subject disclosing her who-ness. 'Hence, when I insert myself into the world', she writes, 'it is a world where others are already present' (Arendt 1987: 39). By acting in plurality, the actor at once enters a worldly and political relation with others, and affirms her distinctiveness from them. As we will see in the following section, it is through spatialisation that this relation to the world and others is established.

Politics as Space-Making

Action has a specific function in Arendt's phenomenology of active life. It contributes neither to life in the biological sense, as labour does, nor to the production of artefacts, as work does. Action relates individuals to one another. It is 'what links an individual to other individuals all similar and all different' (Taminiaux 1997: 28). As we have seen, Arendt's politics depends on a relationship between individuals that is not based on already existing identities or affiliations, but that, nevertheless, has a worldly grounding and quality. Space inscribes action within a common domain (which, however, is not given *a priori*), so that mutual exposure and sharing of words and deeds become possible. This is a new and ephemeral space that cannot be reduced to existing spatial orderings and inscriptions, but it is not entirely separate from them either, because it comes to being as part of the world. What happens in this space, however, 'transcends' existing spatialisations.

In Chapter 2 we saw how Kant's notion of aesthetic judgement allows Arendt to relate plurality, communicability, phenomenality and worldliness, which are the core elements of her political aesthetic. However, she still needs to represent the entering into relationship of these elements. Spatialisation performs this function by providing a common domain of experience for individuals where they can appear to others and others to them. The name Arendt gives to this political domain is 'space of appearance'. The space of appearance is a contingent public realm of phenomena produced by action. This is a space where the worldly concerns of necessity and interest may enter, but it is not produced by them. In other words, the specificity of the space of appearance is defined not by necessity or interest, but by public disclosure and performance – the words and deeds – of the actors.

For Arendt, the universal element in politics is a shared capacity for action. Political action inaugurates space – a space of encounter that at once relates and separates individuals, where the self in her distinctiveness is disclosed in relation to others present. This spatialisation is a sensible manifestation of the freedom of the actor, and the stage, as it were, of her individuation. It is different and distinct from other domains and established institutions of politics. It is inaugurative – allows a second birth to actors for inserting themselves into the world – and inaugurated – something not already given, but produced through action. Entering into a political relation, therefore, depends on spatial formation. The constitution of a space of appearance represents this entering into relationship of individuals, with one another and with the world of things they share. How this world is constituted, disclosed, disrupted or preserved is a matter of politics.

The creation of a space of appearance is at once inaugurative and ruptural, because it not only accounts for natality as a second birth through which actors insert themselves into the world, but also opens up a new space that disrupts the existing order, however momentarily. This spatial term evokes the form and mode of politics for Arendt. It is through spatialisation that a political relation to the world and others is established, and this takes the form of a contingent and ephemeral domain of experience. Politics takes place in sensible spaces that are created each time individuals act together in the presence of others. These spaces do not exist as already given independent entities, but are the products of contingent relations. There is, therefore, no inherent space for politics; the inauguration of politics is concurrent with inauguration of space. While labour gets tangled in a cycle of repetition, and work aims to produce an enduring world of artefacts, space of appearance comes into being contingently and only temporarily. It is not bound by rules of routine or durability; it is an ephemeral space that can be constituted as long as we have plurality as a political relation. As Arendt (1958: 199) writes:

> The space of appearance comes into being wherever men are together in the manner of speech and action, and therefore predates and precedes all formal constitution of the public realm and the various forms of government. . . . Its peculiarity is that, unlike the spaces which are the work of our hands, it does not survive the actuality of the movement which brought it into being, but disappears not only with the dispersal of man . . . but with the disappearance or arrest of the activities themselves. Wherever people gather together, it is potentially there, but only potentially, not necessarily and not forever.

Arendt's emphasis on contingent, rather than institutionalised, spaces for politics does not, however, mean that she denies the significance of the formal public realm protected by law. Spaces of appearance predate and precede formal constitutions of the public realm and forms of government, but this does not imply that they are opened in 'a prepolitical natural state' (Kalyvas 2008: 230). Arendt distinguishes politics from institutionalised politics because institutionalisation as such is not a guarantee of freedom and political action, and no institutionalisation can ever exhaust all political possibilities (Zerilli 2005; Lindahl 2006).

This raises a question on the nature of new beginnings that such spaces initiate. Markell argues that Arendt's notion of beginning does not necessarily imply a disruption of existing orders. She uses the term to evoke 'attention and responsiveness to worldly events' that action involves (Markell 2010: 65), which may or may not be disruptive. However, if we conceive of beginnings in spatial terms as the opening-up of new spaces, as Arendt's account suggests, then we can see that they are about introducing something new in a given context without necessarily suggesting that this will end up in a change of the existing order. The opening-up of a new space is an instant of disruption in any given spatial order, and Arendt's spaces of politics are not opened *ex nihilo* but from within the given spaces of the polity. We cannot, however, know what will follow, because, as Arendt insists, action is not predictable. Actors open a space and by doing so disrupt the normal course or unity of an established order, even only momentarily, to introduce something new into the world of appearances that demands, at the very least, to be seen. So perhaps what is needed is to de-dramatise the notion of disruption, which does not necessarily lead to the undoing of an existing order. A beginning, in the language I have been using, is a mode of relating to the world by actors who are moved by the world they perceive. This suggests a politics in so far as it involves forms of perceiving the world and modes of relating to it.

A beginning, then, is always a beginning in a given context, rather than an absolute beginning. Indeed, Arendt herself was critical of the idea of absolute beginning in the form of a total rupture. As Kalyvas (2008: 223) observes, although for Arendt 'the possibility of a new spontaneous beginning signifies a break from the preestablished political, institutional, and legal order, it does not correspond to an absolute rupture'. Without a context to give it momentum, meaning and significance, the idea of a new beginning in the form of an absolute rupture would amount to 'thinking the unthinkable' (Arendt 1978/II: 208). In each beginning, Arendt writes, 'something new comes *into an already existing world*', and this is where the miracle occurs: 'every act, seen from the perspective not of the agent but of the process *in whose framework it occurs* and whose automatism it interrupts, is a "miracle" – that is, something which could not be expected' (Arendt 1977: 166, 168; emphasis added).

Arendt's Partition

We have seen that, although Arendt's emphasis on new beginnings suggests a disruptive form of political action, she does not argue for a total rupture with the past. She recognises the importance of the law to secure and protect a formal public realm, but her notion of space of appearance, which, as she maintains, pre-dates and precedes formal constitutions, keeps open the possibility of human intervention in a given polity.[8] With her notion of space of appearance Arendt not only emphasises the inaugurative, contingent and ruptural nature of politics, but also tries to avoid the total invasion of all domains of life by politics. As we will see in this section, this attempt leads her to partition different domains of life to distinguish politics as a specific activity, and, in doing so, employ contradictory spatial imaginaries.

According to Lefort, Arendt's conceptualisation of politics was informed by her earlier work on and interpretation of totalitarianism.[9] Indeed, as Dietz (2000: 101) argues, her notion of space of appearance was offered as 'the absolute counter' to the loss of a common world that brought about the horrors of totalitarianism, which disintegrated individuals and drawn humanity into an 'empty space' (Arendt 1994: 215). Thus Arendt's account of action and space of appearance as formulated in *The Human Condition* presents an antidote to the collapse of a common world under totalitarianism. This is what leads Lefort to argue that her conceptualisation of politics inverts the image of totalitarianism, an image that has the following four features:

> Firstly, totalitarianism is a regime, it seems, in which everything appears to be political: the juridical, the economic, the scientific and the pedagogic. We observe how the party penetrates every domain and distributes its orders. Secondly, totalitarianism appears to be a regime in which everything becomes public. Thirdly, and this is why we cannot confuse totalitarianism with a vulgar tyranny, it cannot be regarded as an arbitrary type of government insofar as it does refer to a law, or at least to the idea of an absolute law which owes nothing to human interpretation in the here and now . . . Finally, it is a regime which appears to be revolutionary, which sweeps away the past and devotes itself to the creation of a 'new man'. (Lefort 1988: 48)

If, as Lefort argues, Arendt's conceptualisation of politics is an inversion of totalitarianism thus imagined, then we should also find that for Arendt not everything is political or public. Indeed, it is because not everything is public that not everything is political. This points to a feature of Arendt's politics for which she has been frequently criticised: her partition of active life into separate domains, thus presenting a 'pure' conception of politics that is, in fact, devoid of content and substance. This critique is based on the way she spatially conceptualises different domains of life; Arendt's partition is a partition of space. Although this critique is certainly warranted, Arendt's writings also suggest that she does not always posit an absolute conception of space, and that she was not altogether inattentive to boundary crossings and transgressions, even though she does not develop this theme systematically. But let us first get a sense of the critiques directed against her conceptualisation of politics and action.

Kateb, for example, maintains that Arendt's project was to conceptualise the specifically, or authentically, political. This is informed by her understanding of political life in the ancient Greek polis, and by her interpretation of the American and French revolutions, European working-class rebellions from the mid-nineteenth century onwards, and, more recently, civil disobedience in the 1960s. She believes that eruptive, rather than regular and institutionalised, politics is all the more authentic. And she is particularly concerned with politics 'done in the right spirit'; that is, 'when done for its own sake, when done as display or performance, when done at the behest of a "principle", when done for the sheer exhilaration of acting, of starting something new or adventuring on something unprecedented' (Kateb 2001: 126; 2006).

Arendt's politics expresses freedom rather than a given identity. It is a medium and manifestation of the freedom of individuals who are no longer constrained by 'what' they are. The political realm is 'the only realm where men can be truly free' (Arendt 2006: 104). There is then a realm of political life that is different and distinct from a realm of private life or the realm of economic and social necessity for Arendt. There is, in other words, a political realm that is different and distinct from a social one. The 'invasion' of the former by the necessities of social life signals the end of proper politics. Arendt's position is perhaps best illustrated by her interpretation of the failure of the French Revolution. The problem, as she saw it, was that social matters had 'intruded' into the public – that is to say, the political – realm rather than remaining within the private realm where they truly belonged. This intrusion overwhelmed and ruined the political realm, overcame the revolutionaries, and turned their compassion into pity first, then turned pity into violence and despotism:

> Since the revolution had opened the gates of the political realm to the poor, this realm had indeed become 'social'. It was overwhelmed by the cares and worries which actually belonged in the sphere of the household and which, even if they were permitted to enter the public realm, could not be solved by political means, since they were matters of administration, to be put into the hands of experts, rather than issues which could be settled by the twofold process of decision and persuasion . . . with the downfall of political and legal authority and the rise of revolution, [the people] not merely intrude into but burst upon the political domain. Their need was violent, and, as it were, prepolitical; it seemed that only violence could be strong and swift enough to help them. (Arendt 2006: 81)

She does not argue that matters associated with the private or social spheres do not enter the public realm. They might, but, when they do, they refer to administrative and technocratic issues rather than political ones. This is similar to the familiar and arguably more accept-able distinction between 'politics' and 'the political' that informs the political thought of many contemporary thinkers (although the terms they employ may vary). What is striking in Arendt's case is not so much the distinction of politics from institutionalised practices of government and administration, but the fact that she premises this distinction on the basis of a partition of space. We have seen that Arendt wants to conceive of action as separate and autonomous, free from the interference of biological necessity and instrumental reasoning, because she is worried about its appropriation for pri-vate ends, becoming a mere tool serving selfish interests rather than working miracles in and for the common world. What looks like a distinction about ways of thinking about active life, in both its private and public aspects, becomes in Arendt a partition of space, space conceived in absolute terms as a container with discrete and mutually exclusive parts (the private realm versus the public realm, the social versus the political).

This is somewhat surprising, because Arendt (1958: 190) is also a thinker who writes about the creation of new spaces, their disap-pearance, and the boundlessness of action that 'establishes relation-ships' with 'an inherent tendency to force open all limitations and cut across all boundaries'. Her very notion of space of appearance is based on coexistence and relationality rather than on absolute par-titioning. It implies emergence and openness rather than givenness and fixity. This suggests that Arendt employs contradictory spatial imaginaries, and this is perhaps best observed in her notion of action. Her partitioning of active life into discrete domains contradicts her conceptualisation of action as transgressive because there is a contra-diction between her bounded spheres and boundlessness of action, between the seeming fixity of space and the opening-up of new ones. 'If action is boundless and excessive', Honig (1993: 119) asks, 'why should it respect a public–private distinction that seeks, like a law of laws, to regulate and contain it without ever allowing itself to be engaged or contested by it?'

Arendt's distinction is problematic not only for its rigidity, but also for its implications about the content and urge of politics. If we discard as non-political two of the three domains of active life (assuming such compartmentalisation is possible), what then moves individuals to engage in political action? Where, in other words, does politics stem from and what kinds of issues does it seek to address? Wellmer (1997: 37) argues that, because Arendt conceived of everything that had to do with the material reproduction of society as outside the domain of the properly political, she 'was never able to explain what the content of genuine political action could be'. If material concerns and bodily functions are excluded from the public realm, asks Pitkin (1981: 337), 'what *does* she imagine as the content of political speech and action?' She argues that Arendt's way of conceptualising action looks not only 'obscure', but also 'self-defeating': since action is not connected to any of the other domains fundamental for human survival and social life, it seems 'pointless and arbitrary . . . at best empty posturing, at worst, violence and war' (Pitkin 1981: 337, 341).[10]

Action takes place in a tangible and public realm of freedom with the participation of individuals as equals who are not constrained by the basic necessities of life. Arendt distinguishes this kind of freedom from liberation; the latter could be liberation from material constraints, such as poverty, or from political ones, such as oppressive governments. For her freedom manifested in the public realm through action is different from liberation from something. Bernstein argues that she was partly right in distinguishing between the two, since liberation does not necessarily lead to freedom. However, he notes, 'social liberation is not simply a necessary condition for the possibility of political freedom, but the fate of both are inextricably related to each other' (Bernstein 1986: 125). Furthermore, even if we agree that the social and the political must be kept separate, 'issues or problems do not simply come labeled "social", "political", or even "private"' (Bernstein 1986: 122). Bernstein's point is that any issue of problem can become a political matter, although this is not something, as he admits, that Arendt was opposed to. What Arendt wanted was to conceive of action and politics as autonomous, without the influence of necessities and motives that dominate the other domains of life.

This commitment to an idea of a seemingly 'pure politics' not to be contaminated by private or social life leads Deranty and Renault (2009) to argue that Arendt's conceptualisation of politics is 'aristocratic'. Even if it might be appropriated for political thinking, it still fails, because it does not take into account the factors that hinder participation in politics. In other words, while Arendt may be right in conceiving politics as a shared capacity, not everyone can afford to engage in political activity, because the other domains of active life, to put it in Arendt's own terms, leave no room for the highest ranking of them all – action. The central problem for Deranty and Renault is exclusion from politics; not just the nature of political action and its implications for its actors, but the very factors that affect their access to political action. Arendt's partition may work well for accounting for the specificity of politics, but the way it confines factors that might hinder participation in politics makes this activity look like a privilege.

Rancière (2003a) criticises Arendt's partition from a different perspective. He admittedly shares her understanding of politics as a matter of appearance based on the constitution of common scenes rather than as the negotiation of interests. But he finds Arendt's distinction of the social and the political problematic, not necessarily because it drains politics of content or neglects the vital issue of exclusion from politics, but because Arendt makes this distinction the basis of particular ways of life: one that is capable of politics, and the other that is doomed to reproduction and nothing else. For Rancière, as we will see in Chapter 5, politics is precisely about such delineations and designations that distribute aptitudes, define the proper place of things, and discriminate specific ways of life. But Arendt's argument is not that political action is the province of a few. It is, in principle at least, the capacity of each and every beginner; that is to say, each human being. As Taminiaux (1997: 85–6) observes:

> Action for Arendt is in no way the privilege of a few . . . It consists in the very life of each individual, in his or her *bios* . . . Although each human being has to a degree the status of *animal laborans* – an ascription dictated by organic life – and although some have the status of *homo faber* – an ascription that comes as a result of certain aptitudes – all of them have at their birth been endowed with action not as a result of the generic fact of procreation but merely because all emerge in a common world and have the capacity to initiate an absolutely unique sequence of events.

On this reading, then, Arendt does not see action as the privilege of a selected few. Nor does she completely neglect the issue of exclusion from politics. Kalyvas defends her from this critique by arguing that she was 'concerned more with the political causes lurking behind the successes and failures of extraordinary politics rather than with external obstacles, such as poverty, class relations, international geopolitics, and the like'. She did not consider such factors insignificant, but they 'were simply not directly relevant to her project' (Kalyvas 2008: 191). Marchart offers another interpretation, and attributes Arendt's derogatory remarks of 'the social' to her 'anti-foundationalism'. From this perspective, Arendt excludes categories of the social from her conceptualisation of politics because these are figures of foundation. From an anti-foundationalist perspective, this is perfectly understandable because politics 'cannot be grounded in anything outside itself' (Marchart 2007: 46).

Arendt does not argue that necessity and interest are irrelevant as substance of political action. Her attempt, rather, is to distinguish a 'logic of action', as Buckler (2011: 94) puts it, that is not reducible to necessity or interest, even though these may be elements in a political action. She wants to distinguish the logic of action as the disclosure of the self as a distinct and unique person through public appearance 'even when they wholly concentrate upon reaching an altogether worldly, material object' (Arendt 1958: 183). Therefore, material issues are not excluded from her understanding, but they do not form the logic of action and politics as she wants to keep the focus on exposure in the public realm as the embodiment of freedom rather than as the expression of necessity or interest.

We have seen that plurality is the condition of action for Arendt, and it is in the presence of others that common worlds are constituted. Politics is a world question; what moves individuals to act is a common world. Politics brings them together around it, for there is a common concern (inter-est) and a public coming-together (inter-being). The actors are interested in something common to them, and interrelated in public through action and speech. It is in a context of plurality that individuals act together, creating common worlds as spaces where they appear as actors and equals. They thus experience their reciprocity in a way that goes beyond the rhythms and spaces of labour and work. This differentiation is necessary for Arendt's conceptualisation of politics. As Lefort (1986: 64) puts it:

> There is politics only where there is difference between a space in which men recognise each other as citizens, locating themselves together in the perspective of a *common world*, and social life per se in which they only experience their reciprocal dependency, as a result of the division of labour and the necessity to fulfil their needs.[11]

Arendt's politics needs this common world created through action, which would be 'a truly human world that neither mere perception nor mere work suffice to establish' (Lefort 1986: 66). The mere use of life, for Arendt, does not foster this common world that transcends needs and constraints. Life in its non-biological sense manifests itself in the common world, which is a world 'only insomuch as it transcends both the sheer functionalism of things produced for consumption and the sheer utility of objects produced for use' (Arendt 1958: 173). The new and temporary spaces opened up by action transcend existing orders, but also work to secure them inasmuch as they provide a tangible and durable world, as we will see in the following section.

Arendt's Spaces

The criticisms provoked by Arendt's partition are all compelling, in my view, but they reproduce the spatial compartmentalisation that she (problematically) introduces herself, because they play down the interplay between Arendt's different domains. Markell (2011: 16) argues that there is a tendency to see Arendt's labour, work and action in 'territorial' terms, 'as disjunctive categories into which individual instances of human activity can be sorted, each of which properly belongs to a separate domain, whose boundaries must be secured for the sake of resurrecting and preserving the especially fragile and valuable experience of *action* in particular'. This reading is not unwarranted ('each human activity' writes Arendt (1958: 73) in *The Human Condition*, 'points to its proper location in the world'), and *The Human Condition* in particular is marked by what Markell calls a 'territorial impulse'. Arendt does insist on an understanding of action as separate and autonomous, which makes it look devoid of content.

   However, the three 'conditions' – labour, work and action – depend on each other. Even though Arendt's sharp distinction is a problem, these conditions are not unrelated. Labour allows biological survival, work provides the durable world in which individuals act, and action is never action for its own sake but for a common world actors seek collectively to constitute or preserve. It is true that Arendt separates action from labour and work, and grants it a higher position, but this is because action is what keeps the common world together:

> if Arendt insists on the necessity of action as an activity of a rank higher than fabrication, it is not as in Heidegger in order to distance herself from the dwelling erected by *homo faber*, or for the sake of an ontological absence of dwelling. Instead, this higher rank points to the attempts of keeping dwelling safe, of maintaining a common and public world secure for the sake of *amor mundi*, which has no room in Heidegger's fundamental ontology. (Taminiaux 1997: 15)

This is why Markell prefers to refer to the 'territoriality' of Arendt's formulation as 'relational'. There are, in fact, different spatial imaginaries at work in Arendt's writings on action and politics, and her seemingly more restrictive spatial formulations coexist with others that contradict the former. Her argument that action 'always establishes relationships and therefore has an inherent tendency to force open all limitations and cut across all boundaries' (Arendt 1958: 190) as well as her emphasis on the opening of new spaces of appearance suggest that Arendt does not mobilise merely an absolute conception of space. Boundary crossings and new spatialisations are integral parts of her understanding of action and politics.

This is also why Arendt's notion of action is not devoid of content, because it is about the things of this world. As Markell observes, for Arendt action emerges when individuals are faced with and provoked into speech and deed by questions of how the world between them appears – by, in Arendt's words (1958: 182), some 'worldly objective reality'. Worldly artefacts are relevant to action, not merely because they provide a stable and durable 'context', but also because it is from within this context that action emerges.[12] Individuals are provoked into words and deeds by how their common world looks and 'what kind of things are to appear in it' (Arendt 1977: 220). They act in the public realm not merely to disclose themselves, but also because they are moved to do so by the things that appear to them in their world:

> Action and speech go on between men . . . even if their content is exclusively 'objective', concerned with the matters of the world of things in which men move, which physically lies between them and out of which arise their specific, objective, worldly interests. These interests constitute, in the word's most literal significance, something which *inter-est*, which lies between people and therefore can relate and bind them together. Most action and speech is concerned with this in-between, which varies with each group of people, so that most words and deeds are *about* some

worldly objective reality in addition to being a disclosure of the acting and speaking agent. (Arendt 1958: 182)

We have already seen that Arendt refuses to conceive of politics around a common origin or identity. What brings individuals together to act in concert around a common cause is the world they constitute and share. Living together in the world means, as Arendt (1958: 52) puts it, 'essentially that a world of things is between those who have it in common, as a table is located between those who sit around it; the world, like every in-between, relates and separates men at the same time'. Worldly concerns and interests, it seems, are not excluded from Arendt's conception of action and politics.

This brings us back to the question of Arendt's separation of 'the social' from 'the political'. Perhaps what Arendt wants to distinguish is a mentality or a way of thinking, 'not a particular subject-matter, nor a particular class of people, but a particular attitude against which the public realm must be guarded' (Pitkin 1981: 342). Arendt emphasises the autonomy of action because she wants to dissociate it from expediency and process-oriented thinking that characterises biological survival (labour) and the fabrication of durable materials (work). She is critical of the 'rise of the social' in the modern age, which, for her, overwhelmed action by fabrication and labouring. But she is not critical about work and labour as such. What she criticises is the rise of a certain kind of mentality, of ways of thinking about the world and modes of relating to it, that overshadowed the mentality of action as intervention in the common world. As she puts it in *The Human Condition*, 'to have a society of labourers, it is of course not necessary that every member actually be a labourer or worker ... but only that all members consider whatever they do primarily as a way to sustain their own lives and those of their families' (Arendt 1958: 46).

For Pitkin (1981: 346), what matters is the connection between the social and the political, 'the transformation of social conditions into political issues, of need and interest into principle and justice'.[13] But I think Arendt's conceptualisation of action is intended to do precisely this. It is in the nature of action, as she argues, to 'cut across all boundaries' and 'always establish relationships'. This may not bring about immediate gratification, but political action is about forms of perceiving the world and modes of relating to it, because it is provoked by how the world appears to us, and it stages and puts into relation actors, worldly artefacts and matters. The very opening of a space of appearance where worldly issues are made public – as, for example, Occupy did with the issue of inequality without even formulating an explicit demand – and turned perhaps into what Pitkin (1981: 348) calls 'actionable public issues' is the promise of politics. Arendt, it seems to me, is not after a one-way transformation where 'the social' (however defined) is anterior to 'the political'. What politics does is to open a space where matters of a shared world can be inscribed, debated and contested. This space is opened not in the name of private interests and by a capacity for rational calculation to promote them, but in the name of politics as transformative action and by a capacity to initiate new beginnings – Arendt's natality.

The movement of *sans papiers* was a new beginning in the Arendtian sense: individuals acting in freedom 'to call something into being, which did not exist before, which was not given, not even as an object of cognition or imagination, and which therefore, strictly speaking, could not be known' (Arendt 1977: 150). It was known before, of course, that the *sans papiers* existed as labourers and workers, but not, until then, as actors. The beginning was the exposure of *sans papiers* in public space as political subjects, who had hitherto remained as clandestine bodies. This is the Arendtian dimension of the emergence of this new political subjectivity, which is constituted through the actions of individuals who did not officially exist, but who, nevertheless, presented themselves to open up a space of appearance within an already existing world.

The space of appearance, then, does not hang in the air; it is embedded in other spaces from within which it emerges. There is the public square where the actions of *sans papiers* take place, where they disclose themselves as actors. But this is one of the many spaces there, all worldly artefacts produced by work. Just below the ground, there is the vast transportation system that connects these actors to their living and working spaces. Where are these jobs and where do they live – in the peripheral estates or other parts of the city? They are acting in a country to which they do not officially belong, so there are also spaces of belonging and exclusion. What is the geography of these spaces? They are excluded in a political sense, yet there they are, very much part of the city in which they live, work and act. The space of appearance is but one of the many multi-layered spaces, which finds its meaning and significance within this context, as part of this world. Inasmuch as the space of appearance is part of the world, it is already inscribed in a relational geography of spaces and networks.[14] As Taminiaux (1997: 84) puts it, 'there must be a world before the life of someone may appear'.

Action, writes Arendt (1958: 188, 190), is 'never possible in isolation' and always 'acts into a medium', where it establishes new relationships and cuts across existing boundaries. This is also what makes it unpredictable and transgressive: 'Since we always act into a web of relationships, the consequences of each deed are boundless' (Arendt 1987: 41). Actors not only act in space, but mobilise from space and act on it, because they share and are concerned about the things that appear as their world. They also make space, the space of appearance, which somehow transcends the existing spaces that might have provoked them into action and speaks to the ordering principles of the polity. The *sans papiers*' actions are not about residency permits for this or that *sans papiers*, but about permits for all (with 'papers for all!' (*papiers pour tous!*) as one of their slogans).

Arendt is grappling to represent both deprivation from politics – loss of a place in the world – and the capacity for politics – opening spaces of appearance – in terms that suggest a tangible relation to the world. Space is both a condition of natality, through which actors insert themselves into the world and initiate something new, and a domain of experience inaugurated through natality that puts individuals into a political relation. Space as a form of appearance and a mode of actuality allows her to evoke a relatively bounded yet not an absolute domain that allows for coexistence and reciprocity. Spatialisation makes it possible for actors to experience their world as common and become aware of their interdependence for its existence.

There is, however, a tension in her conceptualisation of politics. As we have seen, Arendt insists on politics as a specific form of activity, with its own mentality and logic of action. Her account of the specificity of politics depends on recourse to a spatial distinction that suggests an absolute compartmentalisation of the domains of active life, with political action confined to a separate and autonomous domain. Although this form of spatialisation allows her to account for the specificity of politics, it seems to contradict her conceptualisation of action that suggests a more dynamic and open notion of space. Arendt uses contradictory spatial imaginaries in her conceptualisation of politics, but her writings also suggest a relational approach rather than an absolute spatial demarcation. The very idea of political action opening up new spaces of appearance and experience suggests that Arendt's spatial imagination cannot be limited to an understanding of space as an absolute container of active life. In the next chapter, we will see how Nancy works with an understanding of space as a product of encounters rather than an already given entity, in a way similar to Arendt's space of appearance. Although Nancy's earlier work relies on a spatial imaginary similar to Arendt's partition to account for the specificity of the political, his notion of spacing as the unfolding of space and time through encounters shows a way out of the impasse that such partitioning leads us into. As we will see, Nancy problematises the opening of space through encounters as a question of being in general, and makes this form of spacing constitutive of politics.

Chapter 4
Politics in-Common

Ego sum expositus: The Originary Exposure

Nancy's work is marked by dominant and recurrent themes, even though these are not always treated systematically. In the light of these themes, Nancy's project may be characterised as a recasting of existence as exposure. By making 'being-in-common' – singularity in a context of plurality – the ontological structure of existence, Nancy rethinks community, politics, the body, the world and art in the absence of a transcending essence or a given foundation, and in the presence of others. Existence is coexistence, and our ontological condition is that of a constitutive exposure to others. He develops this ontology notably in *Being Singular Plural*, but it is also at play in his earlier writings on community, finitude and freedom (*The Inoperative Community* and *The Experience of Freedom*). It is also from this ontological position that follows Nancy's emphasis on sense, which, as we have seen in Chapter 2, is produced through encounters between existing beings (*The Sense of the World*).[1]

A central theme in Nancy's ontology then is the theme of the 'common'. Being is always already in-common in so far as it depends on being exposed to others. Being-in-common is the originary exposure and irreducible condition of existence. Indeed, being is being-in-common for Nancy; it is marked by relation and encounters, though not by unity or fusion. The idea of relation and encounters behind this 'ontology of the common' signals a politics, but, as Nancy's response (2000b) in an interview suggests, the link is not straightforward:

> I should engage in self-criticism myself: by writing on 'community', on 'co-appearance', and then on 'being-with', I do believe that I rightly

emphasised the importance of the theme of the 'common' and the necessity to re-think it anew – but I was wrong to think it could come under the heading of 'politics' . . . Politics is therefore for me, from now on, the object of a questioning that has to do first with the relation and the distinction between 'politics' and 'being-in-common'. If you like, the ontology of the common is not immediately political.

As we will see in the last section of this chapter, Nancy has made attempts to engage directly with politics since the publication of this interview (see, in particular, Nancy 2008, 2011). Before moving on to his recent conceptualisation, however, it will be useful first to get a sense of his 'ontology of the common' and the specific terms that emerge from it. I start by introducing the notion of finitude, which informs Nancy's understanding of existence as being-in-common, as something that can only be conceived as the co-appearance and mutual exposure of beings rather than as their mere juxtaposition. The following section develops this idea in spatial terms, and shows how Nancy's account of being suggests an understanding of spatiality as an unfolding that opens being to the world and to one another. His ontology suggests taking form in the world and of the world through spacing. Being in the world for Nancy means disclosure and exposure, and it is intimately bound up with its spatial and temporal unfolding. After presenting this spatial aspect of Nancy ontology, I turn to his conceptualisation of politics, and show that Nancy's earlier work on politics relies on an account of space similar to Arendt's partition to define the specificity of politics. However, he also develops an understanding that emphasises an unfolding of space, using space to suggest a relational and worldly quality to politics rather than to confine it to a separate domain. In the final section I focus on Nancy's more recent conceptualisation of politics, and argue that his recent attempt to demarcate politics from the common contradicts his fundamental ontology of being-in-common as an event of spacing.

Sharing Finitude

Finitude is at the core of Nancy's understanding of existence and community. It is not, however, an essence, ground or substance. Nancy tries to do away with a thinking of community as essence or as something founded on a given ground or substantial identity. Finitude is a shared lack that derives from exposure to one's own

finitude in the condition of plurality. This is a constitutive exposure that implies the presentation of self to the other. Finitude is a
'specific phenomenality' that needs to be exposed, to co-appear. It
thus 'always presents itself in being-in-common' (Nancy 1991: 28).
Being-in-common, as we have seen, is the irreducible condition of
existence for Nancy, marked by exposure and co-appearance. It does
not refer, he notes, to a common being. Being-in-common exposes
one to the other, and it is in this mutual exposure that they come
into being. In other words, co-appearance does not designate the
appearing of already existing beings to each other; it is how they
come into being in the first place:

> Being *in* common means that singular beings are, present themselves, and
> appear only to the extent that they co-appear, to the extent that they are
> exposed, presented, or offered to one another. This co-appearance is not
> something added on to their being; rather, their being comes into being
> in it. (Nancy 1991: 58; translation modified)

This ontology of being as always already in-common informs Nancy's
conceptualisation of community. He is critical of conceiving community as immanent identity, as in, for example, nationalism or other
identitarian movements. The constitution of community around an
immanent identity, turning being-in-common into a union of common beings, runs the risk of totalitarianism. Critchley (1999b) relates
'immanentism' with the aestheticisation of politics associated with
fascist and totalitarian orders that seek to produce community as a
work of art, a fusion of beings unified as an organic whole by some
common essence. Nancy's idea of community is precisely a resistance
to this immanentism, and the basis of this resistance is his ontology of
being-in-common. Being-in-common exposes beings to one another
in their singularity, but does not reduce them to a unified whole.
It is this mutual exposure that they share rather than a common
substance or immanent identity. This irreducibility of singular beings
resists an understanding of community as an objectifiable, figurable
and producible common being. Being-in-common – as opposed to
being first and then sharing a common space or identity – dislocates
any such stability in that it implies 'no longer having, in any form, in
any empirical or ideal place, such a substantial identity, and sharing
this (narcissistic) "lack of identity". This is what philosophy calls
"finitude"' (Nancy 1991: p. xxxviii; emphasis removed).

Therefore, it is finitude, and not a substantial identity or a given place, that makes community for Nancy. This is a community of singular rather than common beings, each exposed to one another in their finitude, which is how they come to being. If singular beings are not defined by a substantial identity or a given space, but rather by their lack thereof, then this suggests that they are always open to the intrusion of others in a world of plurality. They are constantly exposed to their vulnerability and finitude in their encounters with others. They have not fixed spaces, but rather a multitude of spacings in a world shared by other singular beings. Here we arrive at an important aspect of Nancy's ontology. As I have argued in Chapter 2, Nancy's ontology involves a fundamental spatial and aesthetic dimension by making co-appearance the condition of worldly existence. Being-in-common is the originary exposure that allows co-appearance and, thus, coming into being. Without the co-appearance of singular beings, Nancy maintains, there would be nothing. It is the co-appearance of singular beings that keeps opening spaces, that allows spacing. This implies a spatial taking form in the world and of the world – a 'spaciosity' that makes the exposure of the one to the other possible.

Appearing, for Nancy (2000a: 61), signifies 'coming into the world and being in the world, or existence as such'. But his ontology, as we have seen, requires co-appearance in the presence of others, because otherwise we would have nothing. Nancy (2000a: 68) argues that 'there is no "presence" that is not presence to one another'. Co-appearance consists 'in its appearing to itself and to one another, all at once. There is no appearing to oneself except as appearing to one another' (Nancy 2000a: 67). This not only requires exteriorities or spatial forms, but also shared spaces that allow for co-appearance. These shared spaces are not given, but produced at each instant of mutual exposure. To follow Nancy's terminology, they are 'spacings' – domains of simultaneity and coexistence constituted by being together in the mutual and constitutive exposure to one another.

Thus, Nancy's is not an understanding of space as the three-dimensional Euclidean space, nor is space here simply a 'form of experience' in the Kantian sense, although formation of forms, as we have seen in Chapter 2, is important in Nancy's account. Space is exteriority that gives form, but it is also more active than this, as it implies movement rather than standstill, opening up rather than closing in. It is an unfolding that opens existence up to the world and exposes one to the other. This is why Nancy employs the more active and dynamic term 'spacing'. In the next section, we will see in more detail the role this notion of space plays in Nancy's ontology as a form of appearance and a mode of actuality, allowing him to emphasise disclosure, mutual exposure and creation of a world in common.

Spacing with

Singular beings, in Nancy's account, cannot be abstracted from their spatiality or spaciosity. Being in the world assumes appearance and disclosure in and of spatial forms. This implies that singular beings do not simply exist in pre-given space; they are intimately bound up with the spatial and temporal unfolding of the world. In other words, being, space and world are not conceived by Nancy as independent entities. His emphasis rather is on the unfolding of 'a spatial-temporal event of being, of being understood as a clearing of space or an opening of a world in which beings could be intelligible as such' (James 2006: 90).[2] The possibility of apprehending and making sense of the world depends on this event of spacing. Spatialisation opens up the possibility of sense and of worldly experience, and this implies the presentation of aesthetic forms and orders. Or, to put it in the language I have been using, space as a form of appearance allows for the disclosure of phenomena, and space as a form of actuality allows for relations of simultaneity and mutual exposure, providing a 'stage' that singularities open for co-appearance. Being is materialised through spatial forms and in spaces opened up by the mutual exposure of singularities.

Nancy thus offers an account based on the disclosure of and exposure in a world that is spatially ordered and aesthetically apprehended. Finding worldly meaning demands spacing and aesthetic forms that are presented and apprehended in their freedom. This brings us back to the Kantian notion of 'presentation' that was introduced in Chapter 2. Presentation makes world disclosure and engagement with the world possible in freedom from conceptual determination. This freedom is already assumed by Nancy in his notion of spacing that is unique to each encounter. Presentation allows for this freedom while avoiding that everything become pure multiplicity. It allows for sense in a world of multiplicities, and makes the co-appearance of singularities possible. As Nancy (2000a: 65) puts it:

> If being-with is the sharing of a simultaneous space–time, then it involves a presentation of this space–time as such. In order to say 'we', one must present the 'here and now' of this 'we'. Or rather, saying 'we' brings about the presentation of a 'here and now', however it is determined: as a room, a region, a group of friends, an association, a 'people'. *We* can never simply be 'the we', understood as a unique subject, or understood as an indistinct 'we' that is like a diffuse generally. 'We' always expresses a plurality, expresses 'our' being divided and entangled . . . What is presented in this way, each time, is a stage [*scène*] on which several [people] can say 'I', each on his own account, each in turn.

The disclosure of a 'we' does not presuppose an appearance from an invisible origin, as if the 'we' were already present somewhere but not yet visible. The disclosure, exposure and apprehension are themselves constitutive of the 'we' at the here and now, in and as a shared time and space, in and as a common world. Presentation is an essential aspect of this world disclosure and worldly engagement. By allowing worldly engagement in freedom possible, presentation allows for being-in-common, being exposed and apprehended in a common world as a singular being, rather than a common being. Nancy's ontology, then, has a fundamental aesthetic and spatial dimension for it depends on the creation and disclosure of worlds in common. The creation and disclosure of the common as a shared space of experience, as we will see below, is a central theme in his politics, as it is, as we have seen, in Arendt's.

This is why space as a form and mode of apprehending the common is central to Nancy's thinking. Without spatialisation and presentation, it would be impossible to create a world in common or a space of sharing. What appears and co-appears needs spatialisation as an order of exteriority, simultaneity and succession. Space gives form to and allows relations of simultaneity (co-presence) among singular beings that are to be apprehended in common. Space as a form of appearance and a mode of actuality is essential for Nancy because his ontology implies world-making through spatialisation and relation of singularities. Beings are exposed and apprehended in their spaciosity. This also suggests a capacity for beings to be affected by the co-presence of others, and Nancy tries to capture this relational and aesthetic aspect of being in the world and making sense of it with the term *aisthesis*. This term 'implies neither transcendence nor immanence', but relationship and a plurality of senses:

'in the form of being-affected by, and consequently in the form of being-affectable-by, being-liable-to . . . Affectability constitutes the pres-ence of sensible presence, not as a pure virtuality, but as a being-in-itself-always-already-touched' (Nancy 1997: 128).

Co-presence and affectability require a sharing of space and time, and the term Nancy uses to emphasise this is 'with' (or 'cum'). Coming to presence in the world is inseparable from the with. With at once exposes and multiplies ('Cum est un exposant'): 'it puts us before one another, it gives us to one another, it puts us at risk against one another' (Nancy 2001: 119). This is the condition of existence: beings are not simply with others, beings *are* with others. 'Coming into the world and being in the world, or existence as such', according to Nancy (2000a: 61), 'is strictly inseparable, indiscernible from the *cum* or the *with*, which is not only its place and its taking place, but also – and this is the same thing – its fundamental ontological structure'. The sharing of time and space that is unfolded in the event of being, however, does not necessarily imply the sharing of a common identity or essence. If 'being' is 'with' for Nancy, it is as much about sharing as it is about division, and it is more dynamic than a mere juxtaposition of pure exteriorities:

> If I distinguish myself, it is *from with* [*d'avec*] others. *From with* [*D'avec*] is in French a remarkable phrase: one is separated from or from with someone, as one distinguishes the good from with evil, which means one distances oneself from a proximity, but that this distancing implies the proximity within which, at the end of the day, the distancing or distinction still takes place. *With* [*Avec*], generally speaking, is used to signify all sorts of complex and mobile proximities, and cannot be reduced to mere juxtaposition . . . It is always about proximity not only in the sense of being next to one another [*côtoiement*], but also of reciprocal action, exchange, relation, or, at least, mutual exposure. (Nancy 2001: 118)

The with, therefore, does not denote a given and common situation, but refers to a capacity and a possibility: the capacity for things to come to presence and co-appear in the world, and the possibility of sense. The with, therefore,

> is not in a place, since it is rather the place itself: the capacity for something, or rather several things, and several people, to be there, that is, to be *with* one another, or *among* themselves – the *with* or the *among* being precisely nothing other than the place itself, the milieu or the world of

existence. Such a place is called the *sense*. Being-with is making sense, it is being in the sense or according to the sense – this 'sense' not being by any means a vector oriented towards the epiphany of a meaning, but the circulation of proximity in its own distancing, and of distancing in its proximity. (Nancy 2001: 120)

The with is defined as a capacity for things to appear in a condition of plurality. The ontological project of Nancy has a dynamic spatial and relational quality, eschewing fixed grounds and substantial identities. These are evident in the choice of his main operational terms – 'in', 'with' or *'cum'* – which are not things in themselves. These terms cannot, on their own, provide a foundation or substantial identity. They are not things and they are devoid of substance. However, they *relate* and *space* because mobilising them requires the presence of others. This plurality and relationality, as we have seen, are at the core of Nancy's ontology. In Critchley's words (1999a: 244), what 'Nancy is after is a post-foundationalist conception of intersubjectivity that will provide a non-essentialist "basis" for a critical ethics and politics'. But what is the political element here? As we will see in the following section, Nancy's attempt to define the specificity of the political in his earlier work with Lacoue-Labarthe leads him to rely on an account of space that is similar to Arendt's partition. However, we will also see that this is not the only spatial imaginary in Nancy's account; much as was the case with Arendt, Nancy employs different spatial imaginaries in his work.

The Place of Politics

As several commentators have observed, Nancy's ontology involves a reworking of the fundamental Heideggerian ontology of being-with, and his questioning of community can be seen as a reworking and politicisation of Heidegger's *Mitsein* (being-with) and *Dasein* (being-there) (Critchley 1999a; Marchart 2007; Morin 2012). One place to look for the political implications of Nancy's ontology, then, is his rethinking of community, which, according to Manchev (2012), is the central political notion in his work. For Marchart (2007: 69), 'Nancy's theory (or questioning) of community is *intrinsically* a theory (or questioning) of the political'. The ontological primacy Nancy accords to an existential sharing of and through space – 'being with' rather than 'being' – suggests an opening and undermines attempts to ground community in a substantial identity or a given space. As Fynsk (1991: p. x) argues in his foreword to *The Inoperative Community*, from a political perspective, it is crucial that Nancy 'starts from the *relation* and not from the solitary subject or individual'.

This is why Nancy's community is not 'workable' or producible; it is characterised by the lack of a foundation and of a substantial identity. It is in this lack of communitarian substance that Dallmayr locates the political element, for it implies a dynamic view of community that is constantly renegotiated, always in the making through each encounter. This lack of communitarian substance, however, 'does not mean a lack of bonding, just as the accent on "in-operation" does not entail a lapse into indifference of apathetic inaction. Precisely the disruption or "interruption" of total structures carries with it a political and moral momentum' (Dallmayr 1997: 191). As Devisch (2000: 246) notes, Nancy attempts 'to break with a politics in which a pre-given or pre-supposed identity or substance (in the form of a people, a nation, a class, etc.) crystallizes itself into a figure, name or myth'.

The disruption of orders consolidated around a common substance, I believe, is a common theme in Nancy's work in general, and not just his community writings. This is not to suggest that all such orders are inherently bad and need to be disrupted. Nancy's concern, as I understand him, is to resist the 'naturalness' of such orders, and to expose their structuring principles and the naturalised ways of thinking about them. This, in a sense, is a questioning of how the common of a consolidated order (a community) is constituted – not taking this as natural, but urging us to be reflexive about in. This, in my reading, is the political element in Nancy. Nancy's own attempts to draw the political implications of his ontology or to conceptualise politics pre-dates his writings on community. Morin (2012) identifies three stages in his conceptualisation of politics. The first stage, in the early 1980s, consists of his collaboration with Lacoue-Labarthe. The second is developed in the early 1990s in *The Sense of the World*, and the third entails a discussion of democracy and politics as formulated in *The Truth of Democracy*, originally published in 2008. As we will see in the final section of this chapter, Nancy (2011) clarified further his understanding of politics, insisting more explicitly on the 'ontology of the common' and its political implications.

We have seen at the opening of this chapter Nancy's reservations about his previous presupposition of an immediate link between the common and the political. He has also changed his terminology. In his earlier writings of the 1980s, his attempt was to conceptualise 'the political' by first differentiating it from 'politics', but in his later writings he employs only the term 'politics', and focuses more on its relation to the common. Despite these changes, however, Nancy's understanding of politics follows from his ontology of the common, or being-with, which has been a central theme of his work. In this sense, there has not been, as Morin argues, a radical break in his thought. However, Nancy now seems to have gone to the other end, distinguishing the question of the common from politics, and insisting that the former is not political but metaphysical. Although he uses similar terms (common, sense), the way he conceptualises politics spatially contradicts his fundamental ontology of being-in-common as an event of spacing, as we will see in the final section of this chapter.

The distinction between 'politics' (*la politique*) and 'the political' (*le politique*) goes back to Nancy's writings with Lacoue-Labarthe and the publications that came out of the activities of the centre they founded in 1980 ('The Centre for Philosophical Research on the Political'). The centre's research was organised around the following question: 'How to question (indeed, can one), today, what must provisionally be called the *essence of the political*?' (Lacoue-Labarthe and Nancy 1997: 105). If there is a need to question the essence of the political, then something specific to thinking about politics – rather than the concrete practices associated with it, which does not seem to be the research focus of the centre – must have been lost or obscured. Their aim is not so much to discern certain forms of practices as properly political, but to ask what distinguishes the political from other forms of human activity. This, I believe, was the real worry, rather than finding *the* essence of the political, defining it as an inevitability despite contingencies and against embodied practices. This is where the distinction between politics and the political comes in handy, so that politics as a specific form of activity (however defined) does not dissolve in an 'everything is political', which comes down to saying that nothing is:

> the 'everything is political' conceals an effacement of the specificity of the political. This specificity implicates the political as a space (or as an act) separate and distinct from the other components of the social whole. The retreat would thus retrace the contours of this specificity, whose actual

conditions would need to be reinvented (this is, for example, one aspect of Arendt's thinking). (Lacoue-Labarthe and Nancy 1997: 139)

By 'retreating the political' (the title of the first book that came out of the centre's activities), by retreating *from* the unhelpful obviousness of 'everything is political' and re-treating *of* the political, Lacoue-Labarthe and Nancy sought to contemplate what was specific to it. Within this framework, politics designated the everyday, mundane workings of parties and institutions, whereas the political stood for a 'space' that is distinct from those: an arena or a stage that implied something other than institutionalised structures. Critchley (1999b: 216) sees in this distinction a reduction of politics to the political, which 'leads to an exclusion of politics, understood as a field of antagonism, struggle, dissension, contestation, critique, and questioning. Politics takes place on a social terrain that is irreducibly factical, empirical, and contingent.' Although Critchley's point is well taken, it is still possible to find some value in such a distinction within the terms of Lacoue-Labarthe's and Nancy's argument (while also keeping in mind that it is precisely the French term *le politique* – the political – that evokes antagonism, struggle, dissension, contestation and critique outside the established structures of party politics or government, which is what *la politique* – politics – refers to in everyday usage). There is political merit in an attempt to explore the specificity of politics if the aim is less to distinguish certain activities as exemplary of politics than to keep the possibility for politics open by insisting that *any*-thing can become a matter of politics and *any*-one a political subject (which is how I interpret Rancière's attempt in the next chapter, the Kantian inspiration of which I explored in Chapter 2).

For me the point to be critical about Lacoue-Labarthe's and Nancy's formulation is the erasure of whole aspects of social life from the possibility of politics in the name of defining the specificity of the political, thus confining it in a space that is different and distinct from life. As with Arendt's partition that we saw in the previous chapter, they rely on a problematic account of space to account for the specificity of the political. The demarcation they propose between a 'space' that stands for the political, on the one hand, and 'the other components of the social whole', on the other, suggests an absolute compartmentalisation of social life. Defining the specificity of the political on the basis of such a spatialisation is problematic, because it boils down to defining the political as an exclusive field of expertise, withdrawing it not only from institutionalised spaces, but also from ordinary practices of social life. Nancy uses this distinction in his community writings as well, defining the political in spatial terms and as distinct from 'the composition and dynamic of powers' (Nancy 1993: 78) or 'the sociotechnical element of forces and needs' (Nancy 1991: 40):

> the political is the place where community as such is brought into play. It is not, in any case, just the locus of power relations . . . I do not wish to neglect the sphere of power relations . . . But there would be no power relations, nor would there be such a specific unleashing of power (there would merely be a mechanics of force), if the political were not the place of community – in other words, the place of a specific existence, the existence of being-in-common, which gives rise to the existence of being-self. (Nancy 1991: p. xxxvii)

This formulation seems to me less problematic in its spatial premises than his earlier formulation of the specificity of the political with Lacoue-Labarthe. For Nancy, conceiving community as essence signals the closure of the political, because it reduces community to a common being rather than the being-in-common of singular beings. The political momentum comes from the 'unworking' of community against the total structures of essentialising substances, founding myths and figures, technical and governmental arrangements. However, community in itself is not political. The political is 'the place of its exposition' (Nancy 1991: p. xxxviii). Here we see once again that space provides the 'stage' as a domain of experience with others while also allowing each to space their own being – a space of sharing rather than a melting pot. It is being-in-common with others that allows the possibility of opening up new spaces, which is what the political implies for Nancy. It is freedom that opens these spaces and thus presents itself as an unfolding of space. This unfolding of space signals a politics in so far as it implies a disruption of centred and totalising structures, as we will see in the next section.

Freedom as Beginning

As in Arendt, freedom is a main theme in Nancy's ontology and conception of the political. Nancy conceives of freedom as a mode of being, a modality of worldly existence rather than as a quality or property of beings. This resonates with Arendt's understanding of freedom as the 'inherent ability to make a beginning', which, as we saw in the previous chapter, is 'the miracle of freedom' for her (Arendt 2005: 113). For Arendt, we have freedom and capacity for new beginnings by acting with others in the public realm. It is a modality of being in the world with others. 'A life without speech and without action', she writes, 'is literally dead to the world' (Arendt 1958: 176). Freedom is the very beginning of existence for Nancy (1993: 77): 'No one begins *to be* free, but freedom *is* the beginning and endlessly remains the beginning.' Indeed, freedom is the only way to exist; it is the fundamental modality of being in the world. Nancy (1993: 19) maintains that 'there is no existence, that nothing exists, or at least that no one exists, except in freedom'. Singular beings have freedom because they exist, because they cannot exist otherwise. Freedom is not something to be granted, promised or refused; it must be, Nancy (1993: 19) insists, 'the element in which and according to which only existence *takes place* (and time)'.

Therefore, freedom has a worldly and spatial quality for Nancy, as it does for Arendt. The experience of being in the world, thus freedom, implies spatialisation for Nancy – what he calls, as we have seen, spacing or spaciosity. He resists, however, confining it to certain sites, which is why he avoids images of agora or forum as they suggest a prior disposition. Freedom opens space, which also signals the political: 'the political does not primarily consist in the composition and dynamic of powers . . . but in the opening of a space. This space is opened by freedom – initial, inaugural, arising – and freedom there presents itself in action' (Nancy 1993: 78). In this formulation Nancy, like Arendt and Rancière, resists confining politics to already given spaces (such as established institutional structures) or reducing it to a mere play of power relations. Nancy calls this space opened up by freedom the public or political space, which signifies for him 'the originary space of freedom'. Or, to put it differently, 'the political is the "spaciosity" of freedom' (Nancy 1993: 75).

It is significant that Nancy employs spatial terms here rather than formulating this with reference to, say, political apparatus. Spacing is essential in giving space and taking time to apprehend and be exposed to the other. Space as a form of appearance and mode of actuality allows for disclosure, apprehension, exposure and 'staging'; it is through space and spatial forms that beings apprehend the world and enter in worldly relations. Thus freedom, in opening this space, 'exposes existence' (Nancy 1993: 92) through spatial forms and in spaces opened by co-appearing singular beings. There are again parallels here with Arendt and her notion of space of appearance, which, as we have seen, implies disclosure in a shared space opened up by acting in a context of plurality. Nancy claims, however, that there is a fundamental difference between his and Arendt's understanding of spatiality:

> Spacing is the general 'form' – which precisely has no form, but gives *room* for forms and formations, and which is not general, but which gives *room* for singularities – of existence: the spacing, exposure, or retrenchment and cutting (decision) of singularity . . . This spatiality is not so much a given free space – different in this from Hannah Arendt's public space, which takes the form of an institution or of a preliminary foundation. (Nancy 1993: 145)

The account presented in the previous chapter suggests, however, that there is more to Arendt's understanding of spatiality than what Nancy claims here. Arendt acknowledges the significance of a formal public realm protected by law, which is what Nancy seems to be referring to here. But her emphasis is not on the institutionalised spaces of politics, because institutionalisation as such does not guarantee freedom and political action, and cannot exhaust all political possibilities. Her notion of space of appearance addresses precisely this irreducibility of politics to institutional spaces by evoking contingent spaces for politics opened up through action, and she is very clear that such spaces pre-date and precede the formal constitutions of the public realm with its institutions. It seems to me that Nancy's understanding of spatiality is not altogether different from Arendt's. He works with a notion of spatiality that comes 'before' any space is established. The opening of space is linked to the question of being; being in the world requires disclosure and exposure in shared space in a context of plurality. Nancy's rewriting of the ontology of being-with implies, therefore, that being is shared space as it comes into existence through the opening of a space where beings co-appear and share their finitude.

The space opened up by co-appearing singularities is a free space, not because it is designated as such by some authority, but because it is free from pre-determination. Indeed, it does not even exist as space; no spatialisation has yet taken form. 'Ontological sharing, or the singularity of being, opens the space that only freedom is able, not to "fill", but properly to space' (Nancy 1993: 70). As noted above, Nancy's term 'spacing' is aimed at capturing the unfolding of spaces where 'being-in-common takes place: through this free space where we come into mutual presence, where we co-appear. The opening of this space – spacing of time, exposure, event, surprise – is all there is of being, inasmuch as it "is" free' (Nancy 1993: 169; translation modified). This is the shared space of apprehension: spacing provides not only forms but also a 'stage' as a shared domain of experience where singular beings come into mutual presence, are disclosed and exposed to one another. This is not only where, but how, singular beings exist:

> This stage . . . is not a stage in the sense of an artificial space of mimetic representation. It is a stage in the sense of the opening of a space–time for the distribution of singularities, each of whom singularly plays the unique and plural role of the 'self' or the 'being-self' . . . The stage is the space of a co-appearing without which there would be nothing but Being pure and simple, which is to say, all and nothing, all as nothing. (Nancy 2000a: 66–7)

If we agree to Nancy's terms, then we must admit that freedom, which is our only way to exist, opens spaces of sharing. This is associated with the political because this spacing of being at once differentiates (allowing beings to remain as singular pluralities rather than being moulded into a common being) and puts beings on a common stage. In other words, spacing allows being-in-common as singular beings, which, for Nancy, signals the political. But what exactly is the political element here? What does sharing space do politically? In an essay entitled 'Is everything political?', Nancy (2002: 21) seems to offer an answer:

> Politics should now be understood as the specific site of the articulation of a non-unity – and of symbolization of a non-figure. The names of 'equality' and of 'liberty' are only indeterminate, problematic names under which one must maintain . . . the necessity of *not* accomplishing an essence or an end of the incommensurable . . . At this site, politics is far from being 'everything' – even though everything passes through it and thereby comes across and encounters everything else. Politics becomes, precisely, a site of detotalization.

Politics, then, is a space where centred and totalising structures are undone. However, it is still not clear what puts beings on this space and motivates them to act (*do* they deliberately act?) to de-totalise, de-unite or un-figure, which seem to symbolise resisting total or totalising structures for Nancy. The passage just quoted suggests that Nancy is critical of associating universal values to politics. He thus refrains from suggesting an ideal or a value that could guide or motivate politics. He also does not address the crucial issue of wrongs and grievances. What wrongs, what kinds of grievances, lead to political subjectivisation and mobilisation? There is the usual example of totalitarianism, but, other than that, Nancy is silent on this issue in his own attempts to draw the political implications of his ontology of the common.

Marchart (2007: 81) sees this as a problem, which he locates in the 'associational' aspect of Nancy's conception of the political, and, more generally, in his 'philosophism'. He argues that, although Nancy offers a powerful post-foundational conceptualisation of the political along left Heideggerian lines, his 'adherence to the associational trait of the political' runs 'the risk of portraying the world in an all peaceful way'. In his view, what Nancy (and Arendt before him) fails to do is to take into account the constitutive role of antagonism, contestation and conflict. Rather than prioritising these as initiating instances of the political, Nancy, like Arendt, emphasises plurality. Therefore, in Marchart's view, Nancy goes from post-foundationalism to anti-foundationalism because he fails to offer a convincing conceptualisation of what inaugurates the political. Caygill offers a similar critique by comparing Nancy's adoption of *Mitsein* to Arendt's, and argues that, unlike Nancy, Arendt did not fail to admit violence into *Mitsein* by contextualising sharing in a historical struggle for time and space, which could potentially provide the conditions of totalitarianism. Thus, for Arendt, community is constantly at war with itself for sharing space, time and meaning. This admission of violence into *Mitsein* allows Arendt to acknowledge that sharing, which is Nancy's ontological condition, is not benign and peaceful, but ridden with struggle and conflict. For Nancy, however, 'it is enough to show that community is not a substance, but dynamically excessive and relationally mobile' (Caygill 1997: 26).

It seems to me possible, however, to offer another reading of Nancy's conceptualisation of politics and community. According to Nancy's ontology of being-in-common, singular beings are always at the risk of intrusion from others, so there is perhaps an implicit acknowledge-ment of violence, although this is not clearly or directly formulated. He does not identify a certain moment in the inauguration of the political, because politics for him designates the site where totalising structures are challenged. It is about the uncovering of their principles of inaugura-tion, exposing how such structures are founded upon 'common' values or principles. Politics is the site of the exposure of the constitution of the common. He notes, however, that 'everything that is of the "common" is not political, and all that is political is not in every respect "common"' (Nancy 2002: 21). His political concern is to avoid the realisation of an essence (in the form of a myth, ideal or figure) as the unquestioned common foundation of totalising structures.

Therefore, Nancy's conceptualisation of politics proceeds from a problematisation of the common: 'The political space, or the politi-cal as spacing, is given from the outset in the form . . . of the common (absence of) measure of an incommensurable' (Nancy 1993: 75). This brings us back to his earlier formulation of the political as 'the place where community as such is brought into play' (Nancy 1991: p. xxxvii). As I noted in the previous section, the political resists essentialising traits, founding myths and technical arrangements that reduce community to a gathering of common beings. The political denotes a space, a 'place of a specific existence' in Nancy's words, which sounds similar to Arendt's notion of space of appearance. This form of specific existence is guided by a mode of thinking about established communities with a view to 'unworking', rather than reproducing, them. This is a reflexive mode of thinking about the constitution of the common of the community. Nancy's ontol-ogy of being-in-common demands this reflexivity, as it emphasises the unfolding and sharing of space in the event of being, through encounters with others. The consolidation of a community around a common, therefore, is in tension with the plurality and dynamism that Nancy's ontology postulates. As we will see in the next section, Nancy wants to keep open the possibility of opening new spaces that allows being-in-common and resists total domination of space that reduces community to a mere being of togetherness.

A Sensible Revolution

Nancy calls for a revolution – not a political revolution, but a revolu-tion of politics, which, for him, requires another mode of thinking sense. This rethinking of sense must satisfy certain conditions that follow from his ontology of the common. Nancy (2011: 36) lists them as the following: '1) there is sense only in common (which is different from "common"); 2) sense is infinite; 3) sense implies a differential in values.' As we have seen in Chapter 2, sense is another of Nancy's concepts for thinking existence, and his call to rethink sense is, in a way, a call to rethink being in common in the world. Like existence, sense 'is *common*, or it is not' (Nancy 1997: 54). Sense is thus a sharing of being in the world. Nancy uses the term to evoke sensation and movement, and not merely meaning. A movement towards the other and being affected by the other allow singular beings to apprehend and make sense of the world that they find themselves in in-common. Indeed, this world is constituted in this movement, in the unfolding of space and time brought about by this encounter. Sense, then, comes to presence in spaces of sharing, in the spacing of singularities. It is made in the plurality of encounters, and this is why it is 'infinite' for Nancy.

'All space of sense', Nancy (1997: 88) writes in *The Sense of the World*, 'is common space (hence all space is common space . . .) . . . The political is the place of the in-common as such. Or again, the political is the place of being-*together*.' If all space of sense is common space, and, indeed, all space common space, then it follows that all space is space of sense. There is no privileged space for sense, because both space and sense are produced in the event of being and co-appearing. Beings are in the world together, in common and in relation through spacing. This ontological premise means that, for Nancy, there is always possibility of sense, because there is always possibility of creating spaces of sharing through the spacing of being. Sense is not a given, but the outcome of praxis, always in the making, because the ontological condition of being-in-common implies a plurality of encounters that open new spaces of sharing and sense each time. 'Sense', writes Nancy (2011: 46), 'can only be *in common* (it is exchange, sending, returning, sharing [*partage*]) and it cannot be *common* (sense given by a common institution or constitution, by and as a common order).'

Nancy's political project[3] is guided by a concern about the appropriation and domination of sense (and space) in total structures (state, church, nation, and so on) that work to reproduce it in the form of a working and reproducible community.[4] Such a community is no longer a community of beings in-common, but an order of equivalence and of 'being *of* togetherness' (Nancy 1991: p. xxxix). Against total domination of space, Nancy wants to keep the possibility of opening up new spaces, which signals a plurality of sense rather than being overwhelmed by Sense. This concern is manifest in his earlier as well as more recent reflections on politics. It is for this reason that he avoids associating politics with any kind of sense, figure or value. Politics 'is not the bearer of "sense" or "value", it makes it possible for them to find their place . . . Democratic politics opens up a space for multiple identities and their sharing [*partage*]' (Nancy 2008: 49). Nancy no longer equates the political with the place of being-in-common, but proposes an understanding of politics as the opening-up to sense. Politics opens space for multiple identities and sense, rather than affirming given ones. This is why Nancy proposes a change in what he calls 'the paradigm of equivalence', and the challenge he identifies is introducing a 'non-equivalence':

> The condition of non-equivalent affirmation is political in that politics must provide the space for it. But the affirmation itself is not political . . . Politics does not draw any more than the outline, or the plural outlines, of an indeterminacy in whose opening affirmations can take place. Politics does not affirm, it satisfies the claims of affirmation. (2008: 48–9)

This suggests that politics defines a space that is different from the spacing of being and making sense in-common. Nancy's ontology, up until this point, seemed to indicate that being, space, sense and politics were intimately bound up together. His formulation of this non-equivalent affirmation, however, seems to suggest a separation of domains, turning politics into a sort of instrumental tool to provide for a space of sharing rather than recasting the sharing of space as a political question through the exposure of the constitution of the common. In my reading, Nancy's ontology emphasises unfolding of space and time by the event of being. This is the space of being-in-common where finitude and lack of identity are shared, and sense is made. This unfolding of space and time is also the political element, and is inseparable from the event of being. His remarks above suggest that democratic politics opens a space that is different and distinct from the spaces opened up by the event of being. This is contradictory, because it suggests two different spatial and temporal registers, one that follows from the very ontological condition of being-in-common as spacing, and another that comes once the spatial and temporal unfolding of the event of being has taken place – politics coming 'after', as it were, being. The intertwining of being and spacing that is at the core of Nancy's ontology, it seems to me, does not inform his more recent conceptualisation of politics, and he ends up with having to separate his ontology from politics.

This contradiction notwithstanding, Nancy (2011: 46) defends an understanding of politics that 'consists in brushing aside a "common sense" in order to open up to the possibilities of a "sense in common", or rather, of multiple senses in common'. This implies undoing a given order of sense by opening new spaces in and through which sense in common can be made. The political moment for Nancy is the introduction of a non-equivalence in the established order of sense, which emphasises dissensus rather than consensus. As we have seen in Chapter 2, Rancière proposes an understanding of politics as dissensus that implies the disruption of normalised practices of sense-making, altering forms of perceiving the world and modes of relating to it. Nancy states that he agrees with Rancière's insistence on dissensus as a political moment, because it introduces a non-equivalence in the established order or sense. He argues, however, that the thinkers of politics as disruption have not thought enough about the 'common', which he sees as a question of metaphysics and not of politics:

> When Rancière and a few others (Deleuze, for instance) emphasise as a feature of politics something that is diametrical to any sort of resolution – the turnaround of the event, its rarity, the value almost exclusively granted to the insurrectional moment – there are very good reasons for doing so since it is a response to the breakdown of all the forms of what I have called 'resolution' ... but what has *not yet* been dealt with is the question of the 'common'. And this question is not political but – I repeat – metaphysical. (Nancy 2011: 41–2)

That something *is* requires a plurality of relations for Nancy, because the event of being is defined as the unfolding of a space and time in encounters with others. This is the core of Nancy's ontology of being-in-common. The unfolding of a space and time in the event of being gives sense to the ontological condition of being-in-common, and Nancy distinguishes this from a total domination of all space by a given sense. This understanding of spatiality also signals a politics that Nancy defines as a specific mode of existence, which cannot be reduced to a mere being of togetherness as beings juxtaposed in already given space. It is being-in-common that suggests a politics in so far as it implies an unfolding of space through encounters and mutual exposure of beings. The political spaces thus opened manifest the plurality and irreducibility of encounters, and provide the relational domains of experience where the constitution of the common, and the structuring rules or founding principles of consolidated orders, are exposed. The opening of such spaces that invite a reflexivity about the constitution of the common is not unrelated to the ontological condition of being-in-common.

In his more recent work, however, Nancy seems to separate politics from his ontology of the common, insisting on the metaphysical, and not the political, character of the common. His notion of politics as giving space to non-equivalent affirmations of sense that are made in-common raises the question of where the spaces for politics emerge from. In other words, it is not clear how the spacing of politics is related to the spacing of being, which is at the core of his ontology of being-in-common. Although I find Nancy's earlier idea of politics suggesting an unfolding of space to question established orders helpful, his recent partitioning that assigns politics to a sphere distinct from that of the common seems to me less promising.[5] In the next chapter, we will see with Rancière how the question of the common can be an integral part of conceptualising politics.

Chapter 5
Politics for Equals

The Food and the Prison

> In the end, everything in politics turns on the distribution of spaces. What are these places? How do they function? Why are they there? Who can occupy them? For me, political action always acts upon the social as the litigious distribution of places and roles. It is always a matter of knowing who is qualified to say what a particular place is and what is done in it.
>
> (Rancière 2003a: 201)

When a group of unemployed people decide to create a political party in the city of Le Mans in France, they elect Victor as their president, and ask him to present his views on politics at their next meeting. Not having the slightest idea about politics, Victor goes to a park in order to think, and sits next to a homeless man. He is in luck, because the homeless man decides to give him a free tutorial on politics. Politics, he says, is a fraud, and asks Victor to imagine a prison.

In this prison there are, unsurprisingly, prisoners. But they have not done anything wrong; they were born in the prison, where they will stay for the rest of their lives. It is pure chance, a whim of fate: there are those who were born in the prison, and those who were born outside of it. This is the natural order of things. When, one day, the prisoners start complaining about the shortage of food in the prison, an election is organised. There is democracy in this prison, and the prisoners have the right to elect their director. They elect a director from the Left, who thinks that the shortage of food in the prison is unacceptable. When this director proves incapable of resolving the problem, the prisoners elect another director, from the Right this time. In the meantime, the problem of food in the prison becomes a major issue in the political agenda. And this, the homeless man says to Victor, is the fraud. Even if one day the problem of food in the prison is resolved, either by the Left or by the Right, the situation will basically remain unchanged: the prisoners will have enough to eat, but they will still be in the prison. Politics, he concludes, is not about the food in the prison, but about the very prison.[1]

My aim is not to argue whether the homeless person is right or wrong, but to use his example to introduce my interpretation of Rancière's politics. I agree with Deranty (2003) that democratisation of voice is central to Rancière's politics, but argue that Rancière conceptualises this as a spatial practice rather than as, for example, a politics of representation, recognition or discourse. This spatial practice consists in the construction of the place of the universal – equality – locally to challenge the given places of the established order. The main concern of Rancière's politics, then, is to resist the givenness of place; that is, not to take as natural the distributions or partitionings of established orders.[2] This is a political concern, because the seeming naturalness of established orders may work to endow some the authority to govern while leaving others as the governed. Note how the particular spatial organisation taken to be the natural order of things in the homeless man's story provides a locus of enunciation peculiar to prisoners: only noises that express complaints are heard from the prison, but not voices that question the established order of things, which would signal a political moment.[3] Prisoners thus remain for ever the governed, either by the Left or by the Right, and the actual spatial organisation provides the given on the basis of which problems are defined, solutions proposed – addressing the problem of food in the prison rather than questioning the order that makes such a spatial partitioning seem natural. As we will see, the name Rancière gives to such established orders of governance is 'the police', as opposed to politics, which implies their disruption in the name of equality.

What is particularly appealing in Rancière's conceptualisation is his recognition that space, as a medium of both fixity and change, is integral to the police and politics. There is a strong spatial element in his conceptualisation of politics, which, when attended to, answers some of the ambiguities of his work. The spatial aspect of his conceptualisation makes clear, for example, that he is not after some form of 'pure' politics untainted by 'ordinary politics' because the police and politics are enmeshed. As we will see, Rancière uses a deliberate spatial vocabulary to emphasise the different logics of the police and politics, which usually gets lost in the English translation.

This emphasis on spatiality may seem surprising when compared to some of his commentators insisting on the primacy of temporality in Rancière's political thought. I start with this issue of spatiality versus temporality, and argue that space is integral to Rancière's politics. His conceptualisation is inspired by a rich spatial imagination that accounts for the specificity of politics, and we risk losing sight of this if we read him solely in temporal terms, or with a view of space conceived merely as a fixed and inert container of human life. I then focus on Rancière's notion of 'the distribution of the sensible' (*partage du sensible*). I show how Rancière shares with Nancy an emphasis on the notion of *partage* as partitioning, distribution, and putting in common, but differs in his approach by locating it in specific contexts, both spatially and temporally, rather than taking it as an originary condition of being. The distribution of the sensible, as a particular consolidation of spatial and temporal orders, has policing effect for Rancière, and it is from within these consolidated patterns that politics emerges, as I show in the following section. I then attend to Rancière's use of different spatial terms, and argue that he uses a deliberate spatial vocabulary to differentiate politics from the police and account for its specificity. This is why I insert the original French terms he uses when he talks about 'spaces' and 'places'. In the last section, I revisit the account of *sans papiers* that was first presented in Chapter 3 to point to the differences and similarities between Rancière, Arendt and Nancy. I conclude by arguing that, although all three make spatialisation constitutive of their politics, and rely on a notion of space to convey its specificity, only Rancière problematises spatialisation as a political problem.

Thinking Space Politically

Ingram (2007: 239) compares Arendt and Rancière, and argues that, while the former's 'phenomenological training led her to conceive politics as a domain, Rancière's Marxist background leads him to theorize it as a process, a project, and an event'. Kristin Ross (2009) emphasises the importance of temporality for Rancière, and uses this to launch a critique on the so-called spatial turn of the 1980s in cultural studies. She sees in this turn an 'inherent functionalism' that, according to her, 'affirms the status quo by presenting a social system that is complete, achieved, from which nothing is lacking. Social systems or cultures appear as fixed and complete – fully formed' (Ross 2009: 17). In order to represent the alleged fixity of this spatial thinking, she brings in the notion of 'spatial fix' from David Harvey, and claims that, 'rather than participating in the spatial fix, Rancière preferred to think the way time gives form to relations of power and inequality' (Ross 2009: 18).

I find this assertion problematic for three reasons. First, it is based on a fundamental division between time and space, which seems to me at odds with Rancière's own thinking that seeks to problematise partitionings. Second, it follows from a sketchy and misleading representation of the spatial turn. It is remarkable that there is no engagement with the arguments of thinkers associated with this turn, and this lack of engagement is evident in Ross's misleading use of the notion of spatial fix. Harvey (2000) uses this notion to refer to a survival strategy of capitalism through geographical reorganisation. This involves the production of new spaces (of transport, infrastructure, communications, urban patterns, and so on) in order to facilitate capital accumulation, only to tear them down and reconfigure elsewhere later on for further accumulation. Such 'fixes' allow the system to absorb capital surpluses. Therefore, spatial fix is not about 'fixity' as inertness but about 'solution' to the problem of over-accumulation of capital. It is true that the investments focus on fixed assets (such as infrastructure), but the whole point of the notion of spatial fix is to denote a dynamic of creative destruction that has at its core a relentless process of geographical reorganisation; that is, destruction followed by the production of new spaces.

If space were mere fixity, how would the production of new spaces and new spatial configurations be possible? A whole generation of thinkers, including Harvey, warned against the perils of reducing space to fixity, and the need to consider processes, tensions and struggles as integral parts of the production of space (see, e.g., Soja 1989; Smith 1990; Lefebvre 1991; Keith and Pile 1993; Massey 1993, 2005; Gregory 1994). More recent work has shown that even struggles around a clearly identifiable local issue – so-called place-based politics – are not bounded and fixed, but part of broader spaces and networks constantly in the making (Featherstone 2008). Space, in this account, is neither naturally given nor immutable, but rather a product of relations always in the making. It implies coexistence, but coexistence does not necessarily mean 'completed simultaneity' (Massey 1999: 284) with immutable

connections and juxtapositions. Conceiving space as completed simultaneity is to neglect the dynamic, transformative, conflictual, and thus
political, possibilities offered by space as both 'disrupted and as a source
of disruption' (Massey 1999: 280).

Not only is Ross's prioritisation of time over space, in my view,
problematic and unhelpful, but, as I will show, it is not warranted by
Rancière's own writings either. This, then, is my third and final point
of disagreement with her assertion. Rancière's writings suggest that
he is as sensible to spatial consolidations of power and inequality as
much as he is to temporal ones. As I argued in Chapter 2, a common
thread in Rancière's work is that orders of domination consolidate
or impose spatial and temporal arrangements, and politics is about
disrupting them with affirmations of equality. Rancière himself
writes that in his work the opposition of space to time is 'irrelevant'
(Rancière 2003b: 5), and that his notion of police implies 'a certain
cutting out of space and time' (Rancière 2009a: 31). In his work,
there is no opposition, let alone prioritisation, as far as these two
categories are concerned:

> The issue of space has to be thought in terms of distribution: distribution
> of places, boundaries of what is in or out, central or peripheral, visible
> or invisible. It is related to what I call *the distribution of the sensible*
> ... By this I mean the way in which the abstract and arbitrary forms of
> symbolization of hierarchy are embodied as perceptive givens ... This
> distribution is a certain framing of time and space. The 'spatial' closure
> of Plato's *Republic* which wants that anybody be at its *own place* is its
> temporal partition as well: the artisans are initially figured as they who
> have no time to be elsewhere than in their place. (Rancière 2011a: 6–7)

This goes against Ross's claim that, 'rather than participating in the
spatial fix, Rancière preferred to think the way time gives form to relations of power and inequality', and shows that spatial and temporal
orderings are both of political pertinence for Rancière inasmuch as
they relate to forms of perceiving the world and modes of relating to
it. The distribution of the sensible, as the cutting-up of both time and
space, consolidates perceptual worlds and domains of experience. As
Rancière (2004b: 225–6) states, the temporal and spatial partitionings
thus instituted have been a consistent theme throughout his work:

> This dividing line has been the object of my constant study. It was
> at the heart of *The Nights of Labor*, where the assertion of worker

emancipation was first of all the upheaval of this division of temporalities that anticipated the redistribution of social and political shares by making night into the laborer's time of rest – by inscribing him within the cycle of production and reproduction that separated him from the leisure of thought. It was this that was at stake in *The Philosopher and His Poor*, the Platonic allocation transforming the work's 'absence of time' into the worker's very virtue. But this 'absence of time' was itself only a symbolic division of times and spaces. What Plato had excluded was the slack time and empty space separating the artisan from his purely productive and reproductive destination: the space/time of meetings in the *agora* or the assembly where the power of the 'people' is exerted, where the equality of anyone with anyone is affirmed.

There is no prioritisation of time over space here; both are significant for Rancière, as they help consolidate hierarchical orders. Although I will focus mainly on Rancière's more recent work, it is important to note that this mode of political thinking has been an integral part of his work all the way through, as his quoted remarks suggest. This was already an innovative part of his thinking before *La nuit des prolétaires* (1981) and *Le philosophe et ses pauvres* (1983), as evidenced in the earlier *La leçon d'Althusser* (1974), and even before. In a text written in 1969 and later reproduced in his book on Althusser, Rancière (2011b: 235, 236) argues that dominant ideology 'does not simply – not even essentially – express itself in any given content of knowledge, but in the very division of knowledge', as materialised, for example, in the form of universities, disciplines, and so on. It is 'the very space in which scientific knowledge is inscribed' Later, reflecting on his earlier work, Rancière (2012: 106–7) explains that the notion of space allowed him to elaborate a critique of the Althusserian notion of ideology by escaping the Platonic illusion:

> I said: Instead of speaking of correct or incorrect vision, let's speak in terms of place [*place*]. Let's not say people are where they are because they don't understand why they are there. Let's say they are there simply because they are there. Being there entails a certain knowledge about what it means to be there. But this assignation to a place [*place*] has nothing to do with a structure of illusion.

Space helped him not only to 'step back', as he puts it, from an understanding of ideology based on a dichotomy between illusion and reality, but also to incorporate the notion of coexistence into his thinking.

Time, he observes, is associated with forms of proscription and pre-scription; it 'always functions as an alibi for interdiction'. Therefore, he explains, 'I tried to replace that with space in the sense that space is something like a medium of distribution but also of coexistence . . . What time classically denies is coexistence' (Rancière 2012: 108). While admitting the importance of time in his work, Rancière (2012: 110) emphasises that both space and time are crucial in his notion of distribution of the sensible, and gives the example of the working day as 'lived space–time'. 'The first point concerning the issue of space–time', he states, is that they 'are the essential elements that operate the distribution' (Rancière 2012: 107). This is why Rancière (2003a: 201) maintains that 'everything in politics turns on the distribution of spaces'. Furthermore, his writings are unmistakeably transparent regarding the role space plays in his conceptualisation of politics. He defines the principal function of politics as 'the configuration of its own space' (Rancière 2001: 22; translation modified),[4] political subjectification as 'the opening up of a subject space' (Rancière 1999: 36), and the only universal in politics as equality, the call for which, he writes, 'never makes itself heard without defining its own space' (Rancière 1995a: 50; see also 1995b: 65; 1998: 68–9, 85).

This is not to suggest that Rancière is not a thinker of the event. I agree that politics for Rancière is 'an event that cannot be predicted any more than its end can be apocalyptically announced. It is always circumstantial, local and entirely contained in its singular manifesta-tions' (Ross 2009: 29). But politics does not take place on the head of a pin or within the already given places of the police. It needs to create its own space to 'disclose the world of its subjects and its operations' (Rancière 2001: 22), to construct 'locally the place [lieu] of the universal, the place [lieu] for the demonstration of equality' (Rancière 1995b: 69; 1998: 91). It needs spaces where equality and its absence can coexist (Rancière 1999) – something that requires the medium of space, as he observes. Ross's particular conception of space empties it out of eventfulness, whereas for Rancière space is an integral part of the unfolding and coming into presence of the event of politics. Space here does not refer to an obvious, fixed and unproblematic 'over there', but to the unfolding of politics, as a form of appearance and a mode of actuality. This spatialisation is the event of politics. I agree then with Ross and Ingram that Rancière's politics implies change and process, but argue that its unfolding and specificity cannot be understood without some form of spatialisation.

As I argued in Chapter 1, space is not univocally 'political'; it is as much about inauguration of politics as it is of its containment, as much ruptural as governmental. Space and spatialisation are effective tools of government and containment, but this is not the only way to conceive of the relationship between space and politics. Ross's claim deserves attention in that it shows how one-sided understandings of space may be. The fact that space can be rendered so obvious mainly as Newtonian absolute space (Massey 2005) leads to the neglect of other kinds of thinking space and its production through dynamics, processes, tensions and struggles. Ross's remarks suggest that the understanding of space as a fixed and inert 'container' of human life, geometrically divisible into discrete and mutually exclusive parts, still retains its dominance, which is precisely what the thinkers associated with the spatial turn had tried to challenge. In this understanding, space – static, partitioned and partitioning – unsurprisingly becomes a means of mastery, providing an immutable and exclusive system of demarcation as the basis of and for government – the police, in Rancière's terminology, the prison, in the homeless man's story. The image of fixity of space evokes leads to its association with immutable structures.

It is this one-sided understanding of space as absolute space that leads to its dissociation from change and process. However, this is not the only way to conceive space. Space is not only about bounded-ness, but about openness and emergence as well (Malpas 2012). We saw in the previous chapters with Arendt and Nancy the problems stemming from a recourse to a notion of space conceived in absolute terms as a container – what I called 'Arendt's partition', which is based on an absolute compartmentalisation of life into separate spheres to define the specificity of politics. But both Arendt and Nancy also showed us ways beyond this with an understanding of space as relationality and coexistence, as openness and emergence rather than mere demarcation and compartmentalisation. Informed by this understanding of space, their politics opens up relational domains rather than remaining confined to designated places. Space as a distinctive coming-together, rather than a given container or an absolute system of coordinates, becomes an integral part of the inauguration of politics. Before moving on to politics, however, let us first get a sense of where it emerges from – namely, hierarchical orders of time and space that Rancière calls 'the police'.

Policing Effects of the Sensible

> Where Foucault thinks in terms of limits, closure and exclusion, I think in terms of internal division and transgression. *L'Histoire de la folie* was about locking up 'madmen' as an external structuring condition of classical reason. In *La nuit des prolétaires*, I was interested in the way workers appropriated a time of writing and thought that they 'could not' have. Here we are in a polemical arena rather than an archaeological one. And thus it's the question of equality – which for Foucault had no *theoretical* pertinence – that makes the difference between us.
>
> (Rancière 2000a: 13)

In the same interview from which this epigraph is taken, Rancière describes his debt to Foucault as well: 'The idea of the partition of the sensible is no doubt my own way of translating and appropriating for my own account the genealogical thought of Foucault – his way of systemizing how things can be visible, utterable, and capable of being thought' (Rancière 2000a: 13). As I argued in Chapter 2, with the notion of distribution of the sensible (*partage du sensible*), Rancière links politics to aesthetics as a form of perceiving the world and a mode of relating to it, thus altering and expanding Kant's notion of time and space as *a priori* forms that order what is presented to sense experience. The Foucauldian strand of his thought allows Rancière to historicise and contextualise this notion. The distribution of the sensible is the product of processes and tensions embedded in particular historical and geographical contexts. It refers to symbolic and material orderings of a given community, as well as to its dominant sense-making practices: what is seen and audible, what is heard as a voice or a noise, what is thinkable or unthinkable. The distribution of the sensible denotes forms and modes of configuring a sensible order that makes a certain perception of the world possible and sensible by relating what is given to the senses to practices of sense-making.

Like Nancy, Rancière uses the word *partage* in its double meaning. We have seen in the previous chapter that for Nancy being is sharing (*partage*), and, since 'being-in-common is contemporaneous with singular existence and coextensive with its own spatiality' (Nancy 1993: 66), what is shared is space. In the space of sharing, singular beings are both distinguished as exteriorities in space and put onto a common stage where they co-appear to one another. This emphasis on *partage*, suggesting not merely partitioning but also distribution and putting in common, is something Rancière shares with Nancy.

If *partage* were only partitioning, there would not be any possibility for politics, because everything would be neatly separated and nothing would be put in common. Nancy (2011: 37, 38), as we have seen, insists on the 'essential, even ontological, character' of *partage*, which, for him, is 'the originary condition of existence in general: it is common and divided between beings'. Rancière, however, is interested in the spatialisations of *partage*. As we will see, the *partage* is not an originary ontological condition that is anterior to politics for him. He locates it in specific contexts, both spatially and temporally, and problematises it as the very source of wrong and grievances that demand to be addressed politically.

Rancière (2000b: 12) defines the *partage du sensible* as 'that system of sensible evidences that discloses at once the existence of a common and the partitions that define the respective places and parts in it'. It is 'constituted by a series of discursive acts and reconfigurations of a perceptive field' (Rancière 2000c: 117). His argument is not that such reconfigurations lead to illusionary perceptions, while reality lies somewhere else. His point is that such orders work through what they present to the senses as self-evident facts. In other words, he is concerned about the worlds of sensible experience that such orders create, rather than the falsity or reality of what is presented to the senses. The distribution of the sensible has a policing effect, and Rancière uses the term 'the police' (*la police*) in its original, non-pejorative sense to refer to orders of governance.[5] The essence of the police is not repression but distribution – the distribution, or partitioning, of the sensible, of what is made available to the senses and what is made to make sense. The police refers to orders of sensibility and implies 'a certain cutting out of space and time that binds together practices, forms of visibility, and patterns of intelligibility' (Rancière 2009a: 31). Unlike Foucault, who treats the police as an institutional device implicated in the exercise of power on bodies and life, Rancière (2000d) uses the term to refer not 'to an institution of power, but to a principle of the partition of the sensible within which strategies and techniques of power can be defined'.

The police is a form of symbolisation that consolidates orders of time and space, hierarchies of places, and, through these, institutionalised, legitimised or naturalised forms of governance. It refers to an established order of governance with everyone in their 'proper place' in the seemingly natural order of things, like the prison in the story that opens this chapter. It is based on a partitioned spatial and temporal organisation whose principle is saturation: 'the absence of a void and of a supplement' (Rancière 2001: Thesis 7). This resonates with Laclau's and Mouffe's concept (1985) of hegemony. In their conceptualisation, a totally sutured society, or, in other words, a total closure of the social, is impossible, for there will always be a lack (or surplus), which is what the hegemonic practices are trying to fill in. This lack or surplus makes hegemonic practices possible because hegemony presumes the open and incomplete quality of the social. Hegemony, therefore, is always incomplete, and achieved in a context of antagonism. For Rancière, as well, the police is never a finished and immutable order, and the very lack or surplus in the police order is the constituting moment of politics. This makes politics a permanent possibility, since the givens of a police order, from the viewpoint of politics, are never objective, but always polemical.

From the viewpoint of the police, 'society consists of groups dedicated to specific modes of action, in places [places] where these occupations are exercised, in modes of being corresponding to these occupations and these places [places]' (Rancière 2001: 21). Some places are places of voice, others of noise; work must be performed in certain times and places, public spaces are designed for the mingling of peaceful souls and not for protestors against perceived injustices, and so on. Even 'politics' has its proper place in the partitioned order of the police. This, however, is to confuse politics with the police, argues Rancière. What is generally referred to as politics, such as the organisation of powers, the distribution of places and roles with its systems of legitimisation, the procedures through which different parties reach a consensus, even the organisation of democratic elections in the prison are different forms of governance. Such institutionalised practices belong to the police, and not to politics, which, as we will see below, cannot be institutionalised according to Rancière.

The police is organisation for government, which is achieved through the configuration of a perceptive field as the basis for it. It is perhaps exemplary in this sense that one of the first actions of Nicolas Sarkozy, when he took office as Minister of the Interior in 2002 with a stated aim to 'restore the Republican order' in France, was to modify the periodicity of the publication of delinquency figures, and to make them publicly available more frequently (Le Monde, 31 May 2002). Once the new statistical categories had been created, made sensible and made to make sense, the concrete measures that followed seemed only 'natural', initiated by a government anxious to deal with a situation the givens of which it had redefined by designating police activity as an indicator of security. Rancière's focus, however, is not merely on state interventions, and he uses the term police in a broad sense to refer to

> all the activities which create order by distributing places, names, functions, etc. This means separating the police from that which usually accompanies it, that is to say, the idea of forces of order, repression, the political police and so forth, and returning it to its original sense: the police is the division of the perceptible, which in itself defines the constitution of parties and their parts. (Rancière 1994: 173)

Three points should be emphasised here. First, the plurality of activities in Rancière's definition is essential, otherwise the police would merely be a shorthand for totalitarianism. Thus, the police is not a single dominant power that intentionally and exhaustively orders our lives. Second, the police – any police – order is contested and full of tension. Although the police notion of the society is based on a principle of saturation, there is never a total closure. And, third, the police is not identical to 'state apparatus', and the term does not presuppose an opposition between state and society. 'The distribution of places [*places*] and roles that defines a police regime stems as much from the assumed spontaneity of social relations as from the rigidity of state functions' (Rancière 1999: 29). Every governing system specifies its police. Any hierarchical structure, then, might be seen as a police order:

> The police is thus first an order of bodies that defines the allocation of ways of doing, ways of being, and ways of saying, and sees that those bodies are assigned by name to a particular place [*place*] and task; it is an order of the visible and the sayable that sees that a particular activity is visible and another is not, that this speech is understood as discourse and another as noise. (Rancière 1999: 29)

Rancière's worry is not with the police as such. He is concerned with the naturalisation of hierarchical orders, because such naturalisation of hierarchy works to 'wrong'[6] the principle of radical equality – equality of anyone with anyone, as we saw in Chapter 2. Note how the world in the homeless man's story is based on a given form of perceiving as natural an order structured in two separate domains – prison and outside – and relating to it on the basis of this given partition of places and distribution of people. But, as I suggested in Chapter 1, how this world is constructed, disclosed and disrupted is a matter of politics. The apparent fixity of the order can be challenged. If police orders are consolidated and apprehended spatially and temporally, they are also disrupted through spatial and temporal practices that enact equality. Space is key to Rancière's conceptualisation because, as a form of appearance and an order of relations, it throws hierarchy into sharp relief, and, as a domain of experience and coexistence, it creates spaces where a wrong can be addressed and equality demonstrated from within the police order that wrongs equality. 'The principal function of politics', Rancière (2001: 22) writes, 'is the configuration of its own *space* [*espace*]. It is to *disclose* the world of its subjects and its operations. The essence of politics is the manifestation of dissensus, as the presence of two worlds in one' (emphasis added).[7] Let us now take a closer look at how Rancière conceptualises politics, and what role space and spatialisation play in it.

Inauguration of Politics

As we have seen, the police is a distribution of places, people, activities, authorities and evidences, but the order it consolidates can be challenged. The essence of politics, Rancière (2001: 21) argues, is to disturb the consolidated police order 'by supplementing it with a part of the no-part identified with the community as a whole'. Politics exists when the police order is disrupted, 'when the natural order of domination is interrupted by the institution of a part of those who have no part' (Rancière 1999: 11) – the unaccounted for. This definition immediately raises a question: is Rancière's conceptualisation of politics based on a simple dichotomy between the 'accounted for' (those who have an assigned place in the police order) and the 'unaccounted for'? Isin (2002: 277), for example, discerns this as a problem and asks (quoting Rancière): 'But is becoming political that moment "when the natural order of domination is interrupted by the institution of a part of those who have no part"?' The problem for Isin is that, by 'reproducing excluded/invisible and included/visible dichotomies', Rancière's politics fails to acknowledge that the visible and the invisible are integral parts of the same order, and fails, therefore, to question the very order of things and loses its subversive or transversal quality.

While I fully agree with Isin that conceiving of politics around such dichotomies is not entirely helpful, I think this is a misleading interpretation of Rancière's conceptualisation. Politics opposes the police, but that does not imply that it is the business of an already existing part that is not counted in the police order. It is the disruption of the police order – the sum of the fully counted, rightly named and properly placed parts – by a part that has no part in this particular counting, naming and placing. So maybe a more helpful question would be the following: if everyone is counted, where does the unaccounted-for come from? If space is partitioned in its entirety by the police, where does politics stem from? What, in other words, is the democratic theme in Rancière that would inaugurate politics as a disruption of the police order?

The answer to these questions may be summarised in a sentence: the whole is more than the sum of its parts. In the whole defined by the police everyone is counted and properly placed – this is the police notion of the whole. The unaccounted for does not refer to a hidden group of political subjects that turn up and disrupt the police order; it is at once nowhere and everywhere. The subject of democracy, and of politics, is 'the people', understood not as 'the collection of members in a community, or the laboring classes of the population', but as the 'power of the *one more*, the power of *anyone*' (Rancière 1995b: 64). As Rancière (2000a: 19) insists, 'there is no constant body of the *demos* that would support democratic pronouncements'. From the viewpoint of the police, 'the people' is identical to the sum of the parts, and can be defined with a population, professional categories, or as the sum of those casting their votes at the proper time, in the proper place, in the proper way and under proper names. This 'attempt to find a direct correspondence between the notion of "the people" and that of "the population", defined as an object that can be completely broken down into given empirical categories', signals the collapse of politics for Rancière (1997: 31). The people is not a given political category that corresponds to countable parts; it is the name of anyone, and no one in particular.

Similarly, a political subject does not refer to a designated part of the political community. Politics is the affair of anyone and no one in particular. The only place one finds the unaccounted-for is the emergence of a political articulation, at a particular space and time, an emergence that becomes the claim of the unaccounted-for to redefine the whole and to speak for a whole that both is and is not yet. The democratic theme, then, is this postulate of the redefinition of the whole through the disruption of the police order by opening spaces of politics. Such a postulate makes necessary the following three features about the nature of politics and the police. First, politics cannot be institutionalised. Formally allowing space for dissent, through the law, for example, is useful, but is not a condition or guarantee of politics. Politics is a call of the people for a new order. Second, the police has to be non-pejorative, since any redefinition of the whole will lead to the constitution of another police; that is, another spatial and temporal order.[8] The police, therefore, is not intrinsically bad. There are, however, practices of policing, and, although the police may be sweet and kind, it is still the opposite of politics. And, third, there is no way to be able to say where politics might emerge from. Since political subjects are not already given, they cannot be identified before they disrupt the police order. Politics is an emergence and a permanent possibility.

What, then, characterises this permanently possible emergence? An example offered by Rancière might be helpful here, that of the retreat of Roman plebeians on Aventine Hill. This, for Rancière, is not a revolt caused by poverty and anger, but a conflict over who has the status of a speaking being to make a claim on the whole of the community. Unlike the revolting Scythian slaves, who constitute themselves as warriors equal to other warriors, but who eventually give up the fight when confronted not with spear and bow but with horsewhips – when treated, in other words, not as warriors but as slaves – the Roman plebeians 'establish another order, another partition of the perceptible' as 'speaking beings sharing the same properties as those who deny them these' (Rancière 1999: 24). The conflict, therefore, is not about assessing interests and entitlements between parties; it is, first of all, a conflict concerning 'the existence of parties as parties and the existence of a relationship that constitutes them as such' (Rancière 1999: 26).[9]

For Rancière, the story of the Roman plebeians represents an instance of the institution of politics by a part that has no part in the natural order of things. The act of the plebeians is not a simple assertion of an identity, an identity given by the existing order. They do not make claims as slaves; they give themselves another name, a 'wrong' name, an impossible identification from the viewpoint of the police (in the words of the story's teller, becoming 'men' from being 'mortals'). There is, therefore, a disidentification followed by an impossible, 'wrong' identification. They constitute a new order with another conception of the whole, where there is no such distinction between plebeians and patricians as far as the equality of speaking beings goes. And, in so doing, they construct a space, a polemical common space for addressing a wrong and demonstrating the equality of anyone with anyone, a common space in which two worlds – and the two opposing logics of the police (true identification and proper placement) and of politics (equality) – exist simultaneously.

Spatialisation provides the medium for this coexistence in a common space where one finds together the patricians, deprived of their superiority and insolence that turned the plebeians' voices into noises, and the plebeians, freed from their imposed inferiority that denied them the audacity to identify themselves with the whole of the community and not as a part that has no part in it. This coexistence, this demonstration of two worlds in one that 'holds equality and its absence together' (Rancière 1999: 89), makes the handling of a wrong and the verification of equality possible. Politics, Rancière (1995a: 97) argues, 'is a function of the fact that a wrong exists, an injustice that needs to be addressed'. This wrong, however, is not a juridical wrong (which could be resolved by the institutions of the police) or an infinite debt (as Lyotard's ethics seems to imply), but a form of injustice that is produced by established spatial and temporal orders in their contingency.

Space, Place and 'Place'

We have seen in Chapter 2 that for Rancière equality exists as an assumption to be constantly verified. 'The only universal in politics', he writes, 'is equality' (Rancière 1995b: 65).[10] The political instant, as his interpretation of the Roman plebeians suggests, consists in the encounter between the police logic and the logic of equality through the constitution of a common space where a wrong can be addressed and equality demonstrated. This space, however, is not given *a priori*. Politics creates its own space, 'brings to life a space of commonality that is actually built in the course of polemic engagement' (Arditi 2007: 38), and this spatialisation is central to Rancière's politics.

These two logics – the logic of the proper that belongs to the police, and of equality that belongs to politics – are conceptualised by two different forms of spatiality in Rancière's work. The police uses space to identify, place, order and fix, because its aim is to achieve stability. Politics, on the other hand, resists the places and placings of the police by creating new spaces for the verification of equality when this is 'wronged' by the established order. The police, in spatial terms, is the embodiment of geometrical reason, of administrative rationality, partitioned and aimed at an exhaustive ordering of the whole to be governed. Yet politics takes place by constructing locally the place of the universal (equality) where a wrong can be addressed and equality demonstrated. Spatialisation, then, does not necessarily imply the cancellation of politics; it becomes an integral element of the disruption of the natural order of domination. For Rancière politics is made possible by subjects configuring, transforming, appropriating space for the manifestation of dissensus, for the coexistence of two worlds in one. They constitute themselves as political subjects in and through space, open new spaces of debate, transform the proper space of circulation into a space of parade, or the proper space of work into a space where political capacity can be demonstrated. Space is not merely a container here; it is through spatialisation that politics is inaugurated.

Two features of Rancière's conceptualisation emerge from this reading. First, that he is not after some form of 'pure' politics untainted by 'ordinary politics', because police and politics are enmeshed. They do not belong to different domains of experience, and spaces of politics emerge from within the determined places of the police. 'A mode of subjectification does not create subjects ex nihilo' (Rancière 1999: 36). If politics puts the seemingly natural ordering of space to an egalitarian test, this is possible not despite the police, but because of it. 'Politics acts on the police', Rancière (1999: 33) writes. 'It acts in the places [*lieux*] and with the words that are common to both, even if it means reshaping those places [*lieux*] and changing the status of those words.' Politics thus emerges from within the police order by constructing spaces that are not determined by it. It consists in

> a series of actions that reconfigure the space [*espace*] where parties, parts, or lack of any parts have been defined. Political activity is whatever shifts a body from the place [*lieu*] assigned to it or changes a place's [function].[11] It makes visible what had no business being seen, and makes heard a discourse where once there was only place for noise; it makes understood as discourse what was once only heard as noise. (Rancière 1999: 30)

The second feature has to do with Rancière's use of spatial terms. As I noted at the outset of this chapter, Rancière uses a deliberate spatial vocabulary in his conceptualisation of politics, which serves to differentiate politics from the police and account for its specificity without suggesting that it belongs to a wholly different domain. In other words, by employing different spatial terms, he emphasises the intertwining of the police and politics, but avoids a clear-cut separation of politics from the police. This spatial interpretation might also be used as a criterion to distinguish between better and worse police orders, a point on which his work offers little elaboration. The challenge for a better police would imply resisting the Platonic urge to put things in their proper places, and to keep open the possibility of the formation of new spaces for politics (and, once they are opened, to find more constructive ways than to send in the militarised police, as we have seen in the several episodes of urban dissent of late). The better police, in Rancière's words (1999: 31), is not 'the one that adheres to the supposedly natural order of society or the science of legislators, but the one that the irruptions of the egalitarian logic have most often deviated from its "natural" logic' (translation modified).

This intertwining, however, requires some form of distinction between the 'spaces' of the police and politics. This is why Rancière employs a deliberate spatial vocabulary and distinguishes between three spatial terms: *espace*, *lieu* and *place*.[12] This differentiation usually gets lost in English, because 'place' translates both *lieu* and *place*. However, Rancière reserves the term *place* – rather than *lieu* – for the police to emphasise the logic of the proper he associates with it. Only once, if I am not mistaken, does he use 'space' when writing about the police, but qualifies it with the adjective 'determined'.[13] When writing about politics, however, he uses either *lieu* or *espace*, both of which carry a less determined and more immediately – though not exclusively – geographical quality. The term *place*, which he uses in his conceptualisation of the police, implies the idea of the proper,[14] some form of ordering, hierarchy and fixation,[15] whereas *lieu* and *espace* do not necessarily imply such qualities. Therefore, the 'place' that translates *place* and the 'place' that translates *lieu* do not imply the same thing.

This differentiation is consistent in Rancière's conceptualisation of the police and politics in his various writings. The former depends 'on the hierarchical distribution of places [*places*] and functions', assigns people 'to their place [*place*]' (Rancière 1998: 83, 89), and 'sees that those bodies are assigned by name to a particular place [*place*] and task' (Rancière 1999: 29). This is the logic of the proper that belongs to the police. The logic of political subjectification, on the other hand, involves 'the constitution of a common place [*lieu*]', 'a place [*lieu*] of the universal, a place [*lieu*] for the demonstration of equality', because the principal function of politics is 'to configure its own space [*espace*]' (Rancière 1998: 89, 91, 177). Thus political subjectification

> is a disidentification, removal from the naturalness of a place [*place*], the opening up of a subject space [*espace*] where anyone can be counted since it is the space [*espace*] where those of no account are counted, where a connection is made between having a part and having no part. (Rancière 1999: 36)

Making a connection between equality and its absence requires the disclosure of two worlds in one, as Rancière puts it. Space performs this function as a medium for coexistence, giving form and disclosing political subjects as well as the hierarchical distributions of the police. Space and place (*lieu*) provide a relatively stable domain of experience, but, as products of various boundary-making practices always in the making, they suggest the impossibility of total closure. Politics thus remains a permanent possibility, the established order of the police with everyone in their proper place notwithstanding. Rancière (2001: 25) writes that politics 'has no "proper" place nor does it possess any "natural" subjects'. In a similar way to the anti-essentialist approach of Laclau and Mouffe (1985), but through the medium of space, Rancière frees politics from the ontological centrality – even necessity – of already established identities. Space carries a 'neutral' – that is, not determined by the police – yet generative and transformative quality. It generates a particular relationship to the order of things as a medium and organising principle of politics, and provides a relatively stable domain of experience for the articulation and disclosure of political subjectivities. Space thus becomes an integral element of the disruption of the natural order of domination as the place where a wrong can be addressed and equality demonstrated.

This definition of the political moment as the encounter between the police order and the postulate of equality accounts for Rancière's scepticism towards the notion of power. In order to understand politics as the meeting of these two logics – of the proper and of equality

– the concept of power should be abandoned, since it 'assert[s] in advance a smooth connection between them'. Rancière's point here is to discern the specificity of the political by avoiding the argument that 'everything is political', since power relations are at work everywhere, which comes up to saying that nothing is.[16]

> So while it is important to show, as Michel Foucault has done magnificently, that the police order extends well beyond its specialized institutions and techniques, it is equally important to say that nothing is political in itself merely because power relationships are at work in it. For a thing to be political, it must give rise to a meeting of police logic and egalitarian logic that is never set up in advance. (Rancière 1999: 32)

'Politics', writes Rancière at the outset of his 'Ten Theses on Politics', 'is not the exercise of power . . . To identify politics with the exercise of, and struggle to possess, power is to do away with politics.' He argues, furthermore, that conceiving politics 'as a theory of power or as an investigation into the grounds of its legitimacy' is to 'reduce the scope of politics as a mode of thinking' (Rancière 2001: 1). Politics implies a disruption of the order of the police through the creation of common spaces where both equality and its absence are disclosed. 'Politics is not made up of power relationships; it is made up of relationships between worlds' (Rancière 1999: 42). Let us now see how Rancière's conceptualisation of politics compares with Arendt's and Nancy's.

Sans papiers as Equals

Rancière, like Arendt and Nancy, refuses to reduce politics to governmental rationality, administrative practices or the organisation of power relations. Politics for Nancy implies inauguration of space in and through which the structuring principles of the community are exposed and put to question. The space inaugurated by politics is itself inaugural where freedom is exercised (Nancy) and where a wrong is addressed and equality demonstrated (Rancière). As we have seen, although Nancy and Rancière share an interest in the notion of *partage*, the former insists on its ontological character, while the latter makes the spatialisations of *partage* – as distribution and division – the very source of wrongs to be addressed politically by putting equality and its absence in common space.

This is the main source of Rancière's disagreement with Arendt. As we have seen in Chapter 3, Arendt seems to privilege certain modes and domains of action as properly political, establishing, therefore, a fundamental division, which is precisely what politics is about for Rancière. According to him, Arendt's partition does not allow an equal share of political capacity for everyone. This is perhaps best illustrated by her interpretation of the failure of the French Revolution, and her comments on John Adams's interpretation of the misfortunes of the poor as remaining in obscurity and not being seen. The problem with the French Revolution for Arendt, as shown in Chapter 3, was that it had allowed 'the poor' into the political realm, thus ruining it with the intrusion of 'social' matters where they did not belong. As for John Adams's 'insight into the crippling consequences of obscurity', Arendt believed that it 'could hardly be shared by the poor themselves'. They would either give in 'to the boredom of vacant time' or 'throw open their private houses in "conspicuous consumption"' rather than trying to excel through public actions (Arendt 2006: 59, 60).

Claiming to be seen, then, would not make sense for them. 'However', Rancière (2009d: 341) responds, 'all my work on the emancipation of workers showed me that the first claim of workers and of the people generally was precisely a claim to visibility, a will to enter into the sphere of appearance, the assertion of a capacity for appearance.'[17] For him, these two examples testify to Arendt's commitment to a distinction between two forms of life, one that is capable of politics, the other doomed to mere survival and reproduction. The modern name for the latter is 'proletarian', which originally (*proletarii*) referred to 'people who make children, who merely live and reproduce without a name, without being counted as part of the symbolic order of the city' (Rancière 1995b: 67). It was precisely when they claimed visibility and demonstrated political capacity that the term became a political name:

> The emancipation of the workers is not a matter of making labour the founding principle of the new society, but rather of the workers emerging from their minority status and proving that they truly belong to the society, that they truly communicate with all in a common space [*espace*]; that they are not merely creatures of need, of complaint and protest, but creatures of discourse and reason, that they are capable of opposing reason with reason and of giving their action a demonstrative form. (Rancière 1995a: 48)

This is also why Rancière takes issue with Aristotle's definition of the political animal as a speaking animal – a commonly shared human capacity of speech and discussion that distinguishes them from animals who make noises that can only express pain or pleasure. But even this allegedly shared capacity, argues Rancière (2011a: 2), is 'split up from the very beginning', because Aristotle establishes a fundamental division by stating that, although slaves understand language, they do not possess it. While this fundamental division negates speaking as a common human capacity, it affirms another shared capacity, for there is a 'primary contradiction' here: slaves must be able to understand their orders and they must also be able to understand that they must obey them. 'And to do that, you must already be the equal of the person who is ordering you. It is this equality that gnaws away at any natural order' (Rancière 1999: 16). Politics, therefore, occurs, not because we are distinct in our faculty of speech, but because those who are not counted as capable of speech make themselves count as speaking beings by enactments of equality. Politics is not a specific way of life; it is the affair of anyone and no one in particular. There is 'no political life', Rancière (2011a: 4) insists, 'but a political stage'. Even those deprived of rights, those who are unrepresentable, are capable of opening up political spaces for the verification of equality.

This is precisely what the *sans papiers* did. They were beginners *and* equals; not only did they manifest their equality as speaking beings, they did so in a context of inequality, staging both equality and its absence by opening a space. On reflecting back on the use of the term *sans papiers*, Cissé (2007) recalls that their aim was to invent a new term (although it was not entirely novel) that made clear that their situation was produced by the government's denial of their rights. One is not simply a *sans papiers*, but becomes so through administrative practices, regulations and procedures. This was, in Rancière's terms, putting two worlds in one:

> Our claims were highly political. Our visibility in demonstrations, meetings, occupations, the debates we organised, made them uncomfortable. For 'illegals' or 'clandestines' to occupy a significant part of the public stage was, for the government, more than troubling, a lengthy disturbance of political life, it gave too 'uncivilised' an image of social life. For French people to claim rights, that was acceptable, only just! But for foreigners to do so, and above all *sans papiers* to do so, that was too much. (Cissé 1999: 81)

Rancière refuses, as does Arendt, to conceive politics around already given identities, but politics for him is precisely about the kinds of partitionings Arendt puts at the heart of her conceptualisation of politics. He also shares with Arendt as well as Nancy a mode of political thinking that makes space and spatialisation integral parts of his conceptualisation. We have already seen this with his notions of the police and politics, but this spatial approach is also indicated in Rancière's definition of the subject of politics as the people (*demos*), understood as the name of anyone and no one in particular. Benveniste (1969) writes that *demos* originally was a concept at once territorial and political, implying a common social condition, and not bonds created through kinship or formal political belonging. The root *dem-* signifies 'to build' and 'house' (which gives rise to the Latin *domus*, 'house'). The Greek words *demios* ('belonging to the people') and *demos* ('the people') are derived from this root (see Casey 1997: 349 n. 9, 356 n. 78).

Rancière's conceptualisation implies that politics, despite the possible perils of spatial closure, needs to define its spaces. Forms of political engagement can mobilise from and make use of divided spaces, spaces of categorisation, representations of space, and physical spaces – in short, various forms of boundary-making practices – for inaugurating spaces for politics. There is, in other words, a need for relatively stable formations for democratic pronouncements. Space, then, becomes the place – if only transiently – where a wrong can be addressed and equality demonstrated.[18] But Rancière wants to keep the spaces of politics open and free from predetermination. Hence his insistence that 'there is no constant body of the *demos* that would support democratic pronouncements' (Rancière 2000a: 19), and his scepticism towards the notion of utopia, which would imply a univocal configuration of sensible evidences (Rancière 2000b: 64, 65). Politics implies an ongoing confrontation, not a definite project that starts and comes to an end once an ideal space (and time) is constituted. It implies multiplicities of space and time. It is thus neither utopian nor messianic, but episodic.

Rancière, unlike Arendt and Nancy, problematises the form space takes by defining spatial (and temporal) orderings as the source of political wrongs. Such orderings are central to the police because defining a proper place or time is essential to stability and government. But such orderings consolidate hierarchies that become second nature, which creates instances where the principle of equality is wronged.

Politics seeks to address such wrongs by acting on established orders of governance. Both the police and politics, from this point of view, are inherently spatial, for they are both concerned with distributions – of activities, authorities, functions, individuals or groups, places and times. Such distributions define legitimate interlocutors, make sensible certain issues while making others imperceptible, distinguish voices from noises. Politics acts on such distributions normalised by regimes of governance. It is about the givens – always polemical and never objective – of a situation, not about alterations within an already established order. It is, in other words, about the established order of things, guided by two assumptions: the sheer contingency of the order and the equality of anyone with anyone. Politics implies a disruption of the established order through a reconfiguration of the system of partitionings and sensible evidences. This, as we have seen in Chapter 2, is what Rancière calls dissensus. As I will argue in the next and final chapter, this is the sublime element in politics that implies a change in ways of perceiving the world and modes of relating to it.

Chapter 6
The Sublime Element in Politics

Disruptive Politics

In the preceding chapters, I have explored the political aesthetic of Arendt, Nancy and Rancière, focusing, in particular, on the role space plays in their conceptualisation of politics. We have seen that their conceptualisations involve a political aesthetic that makes perception of phenomena central to their politics, and, thus, requires aesthetic forms and domains of relationality. Their politics is based on the apprehension of phenomena that are spatially formed and ordered. Space plays a constitutive role in their politics that requires the apprehension of the world through aesthetic forms and the constitution of relational domains of experience and political subjects. These three thinkers also depend on recourse to space to account for the specificity of politics. This is not, as we have seen, always unproblematic. Arendt's and Nancy's earlier conceptualisations do this by using space for delineating a sphere reserved for politics. But they also employ a more relational and dynamic notion of space that suggests a distinctive gathering with no pre-given form of place, which implies an understanding of politics as an unfolding in space and time. Rancière's understanding of politics also suggests this form of spatialisation to distinguish it from the institutionalised spaces of politics. What distinguishes Rancière from Arendt and Nancy is that, with his focus on distribution, he problematises spatialisation as a political problem and focuses on instances where the consolidated spatial and temporal orderings wrong the principle of equality.

What all three share is that their understanding of politics implies some form of generative rupture in the established order of things by opening up new spaces. Their politics is thus inaugurative and disruptive, emphasising a spatial unfolding that unsettles the established ways of sensing and making sense of the world. Politics, I argued in Chapter 1, is about forms of perceiving the world and modes of relating to it. How this world is constructed, disclosed and disrupted is a matter of politics. But what is the nature of disruption when politics is conceived in such aesthetic and spatial terms? If aesthetic forms and spatial distributions are necessary for sensing and making sense of the world, what does politics introduce to disturb them?

In this chapter I suggest that the aesthetic features associated with the sublime offer a way of interpreting disruption in an aesthetic and spatial understanding of politics. This is why I associate politics with the aesthetic features of the Kantian sublime in this chapter, and argue that the disruption of our forms of perceiving the world and modes of relating to it is the sublime element in politics in so far as it unsettles our habitual and normalised ways of sensing and making sense of the world. Therefore, I focus on the aesthetic features of the sublime because it evokes phenomena that cannot initially find a register within our given coordinates and habitual ways of making sense of things.

The emphasis on disruption, however, still needs to be accounted for. One of the lessons I take from these three thinkers is that getting caught up in the normalised practices and repetitive structures of everyday life does not provide the political stimulation to stop and think reflexively about the ordering principles and established practices of political communities. Since, as these thinkers suggest, the common world is constituted and disclosed through spatial forms, it is politically desirable to allow for episodes of disruption to stop and think about its spatial and temporal orderings. Disruptive politics invites reflexivity about the givens of our situation, a reflective withdrawal from the normalised spaces and practices by opening up new spaces. This stop-and-think, as Arendt would have put it, does not suggest a withdrawal from the world, but engagement with it in a reflexive way, exposing and questioning its constitution of the common and ordering principles, as Nancy insists.

The sublime element in politics interrupts repetitive and normalised practices of everyday life within which we risk getting caught up and producing predictable reactions within the routine of our everyday lives. I use the sublime to evoke an image of the disruption, even perhaps subversion, of the ordinary, habitual and unreflexive practices associated with consolidated spatial and temporal orders. I propose to think of disruption as something that looks surprising and unsettling – if not entirely astonishing or outright terrifying – within the given and normalised ways of perceiving the world and making sense of it. Therefore, I use the image of the sublime to evoke a spatial and temporal unfolding that unsettles consolidated spatial and temporal orders, ways of perceiving and modes of relating to them.

In what follows, I first revisit Arendt's 'aestheticisation of politics' through her critics to underline the perils of an unconditional emphasis on disruption for disruption's sake. I then offer an interpretation of disruption, and argue that the disruption of our forms of perceiving the world and modes of relating to it is the sublime element in politics. The introduction of this element alters ways of sensing and making sense of the world, which, however, may characterise the institution of a totalitarian regime as much as it does the disruption of politics. What distinguishes the latter, however, is that it is inaugurated in the name of, and to verify the equality of, anyone with anyone, as Rancière insists in his conceptualisation of politics.

Perils of Disruption

As we have seen in Chapter 2, Kant develops an understanding of aesthetics that is based on the postulate that the ability to make aesthetic judgements is universally shared. We all have the capacity to judge things as beautiful or sublime. Arendt is attracted to judgements concerning the former rather than the latter. She is interested in Kant's notion of judgements of the beautiful for its implications of communicability, plurality and the creation of common worlds. These suggest an understanding of politics that is based on 'getting into community with others' through *sensus communis*, while eschewing the imposition of any rules, standards or truth claims – anything, in short, that compels assent or coerces consensus. Inspired only by the beautiful, however, Arendt's politics is almost too orderly for Cascardi. He argues that Arendt's understanding of aesthetic judgement 'recoils from the sublime', and thus neglects those instances where we are overwhelmed by the presentation of the unpresentable, where the limits of common sense and representation are exceeded (Cascardi 1997: 111). In Cascardi's view (1997: 126), the implications of this exclusion of the sublime are dramatic for Arendt's politics:

To understand the task of politics as ensuring normativity through representability is admittedly to weaken its transformative potential and to risk rendering unintelligible the question of founding. By contrast, to view politics as 'aesthetic' only insofar as it depends upon the representation of ideals that are available only to the creative genius is to risk the legislative arbitrariness that Arendt so deeply feared.

There is, therefore, no disruption in Arendt's politics. Cascardi's argument is that by privileging the Kantian notion of the beautiful over the sublime, Arendt fails to propose a 'politics of radical transformation', and offers a sort of politics that is somewhere between rational communication and normalisation. But this unconditional privileging of the sublime and of disruption leads to two major difficulties. First, it polarises the beautiful and the sublime, communicative politics and transformative politics, to such an extent that we either have one or the other. Cascardi seems to assume that 'consensus is always bad and its disruption is always good' (Fraser 1997: 168), valorising disruption and transformation for their own sake. However, as Fraser (1997: 168–9) puts it, it is 'plainly false' to assume that disruption is always good:

> It is one thing to disrupt a consensus that sees nothing unacceptable in, say, marital rape, and another to disrupt a consensus to the contrary. In the first case, the consensus is unjust and its disruption is a step toward justice; in the second, just the opposite is true.

The second difficulty arises from Cascardi's unconditional valorisation of unrepresentability. He argues that Arendtian politics ends up being all too rational because she avoids the sublime, and thus fails to take into consideration that which exceeds representation. It is politically important to take into consideration what or who can or cannot be represented, but there is nothing in Arendt that prevents this. Cascardi, however, is interested in what is beyond representation. 'An idea', Fraser (1997: 169) responds, 'that resists *all possible* representation has an air of surplus paradox suited better to religion than to politics.' As we will see later on, this idea of sublime unrepresentability is also what Lyotard finds appealing in Kant's theory of aesthetic judgement.

Jay (1997) shares Fraser's doubts about the emancipatory potential of an understanding of politics conceived around an aesthetics of sublime unrepresentability as defined by Cascardi. Arendt herself held that thinking politically was a representative practice as it involved making present to one's mind the standpoints of those who are not present. While Jay is extremely troubled by Cascardi's argument for a sublime aestheticisation of politics, he is not too comfortable with Arendt's more restrained aestheticisation of politics either. The link between aestheticisation of politics and violence, he argues, recalls 'memories of totalitarian and fascist politics' (Cascardi 1997: 342), although we have seen in the introduction that this is not the only implication of relating aesthetics and politics.

We have seen in Chapter 3 that Arendt resists curtailing action by any given standards or truth claims. This leads Kateb to argue that her conception of action is amoral in that it deliberately excludes moral standards guiding or restraining it. This amoral conception of action is not unrelated to her aestheticisation of politics. In trying to free politics from abstract, universal truths, Arendt subordinates morality to aesthetics. 'Aestheticized politics is pure politics, politics for the sake of politics – politics purified, to a considerable extent, from moral anxiety as well as moral goals, just as other aesthetic phenomena are held ideally to be' (Kateb 2001: 122). Although this aspect of Arendt's politics raises concern – for its disjunction from morality, rationality, and for its historical affinity with fascist ideology – it is also what makes her politics creative and disruptive. This is what Kateb (2001: 124) calls 'Arendt's political aestheticism', which he illustrates through the example of artworks:

> Artworks are expressions of a distinctive human capacity: to do something new, creative, unexpected, eruptive, interruptive of routinized perception and response. Although rules and discipline enter into the making of art, art is far more than rules or discipline. Art is the freedom of humanity.

Kateb's illustration brings us closer to another political thinker, whose understanding of politics is decidedly aesthetic, though in a radically different way than the 'aestheticisation of politics' thesis suggests. Inspired by Kant in many ways, Rancière proposes an understanding of politics based on dissensus, the aesthetic features of which I associate with the Kantian sublime in its disruption of 'routinised perception and response'. What I find helpful in Rancière's conceptualisation is that he avoids valorising disruption for its own sake by putting equality at the core of his politics and focusing on instances where equality is wronged by established aesthetic regimes.

Sublime Disruption

As I have argued in Chapter 2, Rancière establishes a relation between Kant's 'two aesthetics'; that is, between forms of perceiving the world – the forms in and through which we perceive worldly phenomena – and modes of relating to the world, to what is presented to our senses. The disruption of established forms of perceiving the world and modes of relating to it implies dissensus, the essence of politics for Rancière (2004c: 304):

> A dissensus is not a conflict of interests, opinions, or values; it is a division put in the 'common sense': a dispute about what is given, about *the frame* within which we see something as given . . . This is what I call a dissensus; putting two worlds in one and the same world. A political subject, as I understand it, is a capacity for staging such scenes of dissensus. (emphasis added)

'Common sense' is qualified because it is not used to refer to a shared capacity that renders aesthetic judgements universally communicable, allowing one 'to get into community with others', as Arendt interpreted Kant. What is implied here is what is commonly made available to the senses and made to make sense – 'the frame', as it were, that conditions forms of perceiving the world and modes of relating to it. The disruption of this 'frame', the alteration of established ways of knowing the world and of worldly involvement, is the sublime element in politics. But what happens at this moment of disruption?

Panagia relates Rancière to Burke, and emphasises astonishment. He argues that 'Rancière's image of political thought is indebted to a Burkean account of the sublime' (Panagia 2006: 16). What drives his interpretation is Burke's emphasis on astonishment. At the moment of our encounter with the sublime, we are faced with an almost unrepresentable element that we cannot grasp, which produces a feeling of astonishment:

> The passion caused by the great and sublime in *nature*, when those causes operate most powerfully, is Astonishment; and astonishment is that state of the soul, in which all its motions are suspended, with some degree of horror. In this case the mind is so entirely filled with its object, that it cannot entertain any other, nor by consequence reason on that object which employs it. (Burke 1998: 101)

The sublime comes as an interruption, filling the mind with astonishment and terror, and throws us back to 'an antisocial state of radical individuality', so radical that 'it forces us to confront our own mortality' (Panagia 2006: 86). For Burke, Panagia goes on to argue, this antisocial state brought about by the sublime experience was a threat for it instilled division. Rancière's politics, on the other hand, is not afraid of division; it is, indeed, divisive itself as it is meant to introduce dissensus. Based on this element of division and the implications of unrepresentability, Panagia concludes that the Burkean account of the sublime and Rancière's account of politics share the same aesthetic features.

Rather than emphasising astonishment, I focus on dissensus as a disagreement occasioned at the moment of encounter with the sublime, and relate politics to the aesthetic features associated with the Kantian sublime. In Kant, too, we are overwhelmed by the power and magnitude of the sublime; the imagination is overcome, as it cannot take in and give form to what is presented to the senses. This leads to a rupture in the hierarchical workings of the understanding and the imagination, which is a general feature of aesthetic experience, not just of the sublime, for Kant.[1] In the sublime, however, this is a call to reason, for we are overwhelmed with what is presented to our senses. For Eagleton (1990: 90) this is not good news:

> Both of these operations, the beautiful and the sublime, are in fact essential dimensions of ideology. For one problem of all humanist ideology is how its centring and consoling of the subject is to be made compatible with a certain essential reverence and submissiveness on the subject's part . . . The sublime in one of its aspects is exactly this chastening, humiliating power, which decentres the subject into an awesome awareness of its finitude, its own petty position in the universe, just as the experience of beauty shores it up.

But Kant was very clear on this, referring to nature in the sublime experience as 'a power that has no dominion over us' (CJ §28). The moral significance of the sublime does not lie in inflicting feelings of humiliation, submissiveness and reverence in the subject through terror, but in showing the subject that, even when nature is at its most mighty, it cannot defeat our capacity to act freely. Therefore, the sublime experience is not about humiliation before a mighty power, but about freedom and autonomy even when faced with such a power. As Bowie puts is, what the sublime does is 'to remind us of the limitations of our *sensuous* relationship to nature'. But it is not merely about limitations; the initial feeling of terror induced by the might of nature eventually elevates our capacity for reason. 'Because we feel our limits of imagination we must *also* feel what is not limited in ourselves . . . Freedom emerges from a situation which seems empirically to be nothing but constraint' (Bowie 2003: 44). Guyer (1996: 264) is quite categorical here: 'the experience of the sublime is not an experience of humility, but an experience of freedom'.

However, this is not the path I want to pursue. While acknowledging the moral implications of the sublime for Kant, I wish to focus on its aesthetic features. This, it seems to me, is not an altogether unreasonable venture. As Gasché (2003: 154) argues, 'even though the sublime remains within aesthetics . . . it gestures towards something else, namely, practical reason and morality. Nevertheless, privileging the sublime on these grounds would do violence to the Kantian conceptuality and uproot the sublime from the aesthetics to which it belongs.'

For Rancière, the political pertinence of aesthetic experience comes from the dissensus it occasions – a disagreement between the understanding and the imagination, between thought and the sensible. This makes 'aesthetic experience to be politically significant – that is, to be more than a Kantian "common sense" promising to bridge the gap between the refinement of the elite and the simplicity of the lower class' (Rancière 2004d: 12). Rancière is alluding here to §29 of the third Critique, where Kant tries to establish the grounds for the subjective necessity of the judgements of the sublime, so that we have a ground for the uncoerced assent of others for our judgement. Kant presumes that we can claim necessity for such judgements, and this is why the sublime is part of his transcendental philosophy. In principle, therefore, all humans share the *a priori* conditions for making judgements of the sublime, as they do for judgements of the beautiful. What is peculiar about the sublime is that these universally shared conditions need to be mediated – or, better yet, cultivated – by 'culture'. As Kant (*CJ* §29) puts it:

> In fact, without the development of moral ideas, that which we, prepared by culture, call sublime will appear merely repellent to the unrefined person. He will see in the proofs of the dominion of nature given by its destructiveness and in the enormous measure of its power, against which

his own vanishes away to nothing, only the distress, danger, and need that would surround the person who was banished thereto. Thus the good and otherwise sensible Savoyard peasant . . . had no hesitation in calling all devotees of the icy mountains fools.

Despite this requirement of culture for judgements of the sublime, however, Kant is careful to note that 'it has its foundations in human nature' and this is the ground for necessity. Culture is required in judgements of sublime, but such judgements are not 'generated' by it (*CJ* §29). As Hughes (2010: 91) explains:

A feeling of the sublime, although based on the rational capacity for principled action present in all human beings whether civilized or not, requires a certain cultivation of both our aesthetic and cognitive powers. Culture helps us develop our rational capacity for ideas and to recognize that it is possible to resist nature. Only once we have been educated to develop this capacity are we in a position to fully appreciate the sublime within us.

Therefore, judgements of the sublime imply subjective necessity, but their claim on the assent of others requires this mediation by culture. Shapiro (2006) argues that Kant turns to such an idea of culture because he realises that the subjective necessity he attributes to judgements of taste and the whole idea of *sensus communis* is imperilled by the sublime. The encounter with the sublime challenges the idea of a naturally given and universally shared common sense, because it disrupts what Kant seeks to establish: a coherent and universal locus from which the world of phenomena is synthesised. In this sense, the political implications of the third Critique lies in

Kant's discovery of the fragility of his synthesis – his reluctant recognition that there is no single place from which to partition the sensible world . . . His inability to establish the subjective necessity he sought, when he evoked the encounter with the sublime, opens up the possibility of a plurality of loci of enunciation and thereby challenges the institutionalised perspectives that dominate those reigning political discourses that depend for their cogency on naturalising or rendering necessary contingent modes of facticity. (Shapiro 2006: 669)

This implies, in the language I have been using, not one but multiple ways of perceiving, relating to and making sense of the world. Shapiro's interpretation is informed by Deleuze's account of the

Kantian synthesis – and its fragility faced with the sublime. What Kant calls 'synthesis', Deleuze (1978a) explains, puts conceptual forms and spatio-temporal forms into a certain relation. Synthesis, in other words, refers the object of our perception to a concept. This is a synthesis of perception, which is necessary for us to know and relate to the world, because it allows us to synthesise the manifold of sensory data we receive, giving them a 'form', a certain spatiality and temporality. Otherwise, it would be pure multiplicity. The synthesis allows us to make sense of the world of phenomena.

Three operations take place before the synthesis is complete: apprehension, reproduction and recognition. We start, Kant believes, with apprehension as we are given a multiplicity of things, which are themselves multiplicities of parts to be successively apprehended. Through this process, we 'take in' the parts of a given phenomenon. Since the parts are successively apprehended, it will be necessary somehow to bring them together, as if bringing together the pieces of a jigsaw puzzle. The apprehension of the parts is therefore followed by the reproduction of the parts by the imagination. We now have a form of space and time, but something else is missing – something that should allow me to say of this form 'it's *this*'. I have apprehended the manifold presented to my senses, reproduced or 'represented' it in the imagination, but not yet related it to an object. A third operation, recognition, completes the process. This is the task of the understanding, which provides the concepts so that I can say: this is an elephant, this is a cat . . . The spatio-temporal form is referred to a conceptual form, and the synthesis is now complete. Without the synthesis, I would have nothing but pure multiplicity, and would not be able to make sense of the world of phenomena. But there are moments when the 'whole structure of perception is in the process of exploding'. This is the encounter with the sublime:

> I can no longer apprehend parts, I can no longer reproduce parts, and finally I can no longer recognize something, and in effect the sublime, as Kant says, is the formless and the deformed. It is the infinite as encompassing all of space, or the infinite as overturning all of space; if my synthesis of perception is suppressed, this is because my *aesthetic comprehension* is itself compromised. (Deleuze 1978a; emphasis added)

Imagination is faced with its limits; it can no longer master the form of the object presented to the senses. Aesthetic comprehension, however, is not merely a part of the synthesis described above; it is 'the basis that the synthesis rests on', not its ground, but its very foundation. What Kant discovers in the third Critique is the fragility of this foundation, since 'the sublime threatens at each instant to overwhelm the imagination's act of synthesis' (Deleuze 1978b).

We have already seen in Chapter 2 that, ordinarily, there is a hierarchical relationship between the imagination and the understanding, where the former operates under the rules of the latter to synthesise the multiplicity of sensory data. The Kantian synthesis – the Kantian way of knowing the world – has to abide by certain temporal and spatial rules: *successive* apprehension of sensory data and *subsumption* under concepts. It is, in this sense, a 'police' – a form and mode of governing the distribution of the sensible, working in an orderly, hierarchical way. It is a form and mode of spatialisation, where spatialisation refers to giving both a spatial form (representation) and placement (recognition); that is, subsumption under a concept. What the sublime encounter disrupts is the ordinary workings of this police by introducing an element that overwhelms it. The sublime 'defies all subsumption under the powers of cognition' as it involves 'a representation that is infinitely rebellious against all cognition' (Gasché 2003: 125). What is disrupted, then, is our ordinary forms of perceiving the world and modes of relating to it, and this, I argue, is the sublime element in politics

Evoking the image of the sublime raises questions regarding unrepresentability and the nature of disruption. I do not seek, as Lyotard does, to transform sublime unrepresentability into an ethical imperative informed by the radical unrepresentability of the other.[2] Nor do I endorse an understanding of politics that privileges disruption for its own sake. We have already seen the limits and perils of such an understanding above – a sort of touch-and-go politics that could end up in a wide spectrum ranging from emancipation to totalitarianism. By associating politics with the aesthetic features of the sublime, I seek to cast as political the disruption of inherited, habitual, routinised or 'common sense' ways of perceiving and making sense of the world by political subjects in the name of equality. These subjects come as excess, as the *sans papiers* did, to the given coordinates of sense-making. The image of the sublime allows me to evoke the unrepresentability of political subjects qua political subjects before they disturb the established order. I endorse, therefore, an understanding of politics animated not by a categorical resistance to all possible representation, but by an openness to unrepresent-ability in so far as it implies that there are no given, 'natural' political subjects. Thus, what I try to capture with the image of the sublime is the non-exhaustiveness of political subjects in established orders of representation, rather than an unconditional valorisation of ulti-mate unrepresentability. The sublime element in politics ensures that political subjects and political spaces are not exhausted by established orders and habitual ways of perceiving the world and relating to it.

Notes

Chapter 1

1. The reference is to the first English translation. The original article was published in French in 1970.
2. See Dikeç (2012) for an earlier formulation of this notion. Note, however, that the present formulation no longer depends on a clear-cut separation between the literal and the metaphorical, a separation that is neither simple nor unproblematic, as Malpas (2012) shows.
3. There is a long tradition in Anglophone geography of this argument since the 1980s, inspired mainly by Lefebvre's writings from the 1970s. I will come back to this in Chapter 5 when discussing Kristin Ross's critique of the so-called spatial turn to which this tradition gave rise.
4. The edition I am using translates the title of the third Critique as *Critique of the Power of Judgment*. In the text, however, I will refer to it as *Critique of Judgment*, as it is more commonly known.
5. Jay identifies three strands. The first uses the term aesthetic to define an autonomous and disinterested realm of art from which non-aesthetic criteria are deliberately excluded – art for art's sake, in short. Politics aestheticised in this sense puts aesthetic worth and radical disinterestedness over human life and interests, an extreme example of which would be Mussolini's son-in-law's admiration of the beauty of the bombs dropped on Ethiopians, comparing them to flowers bursting into bloom. Partly related to this, a second use of the term aesthetic in association with politics reflects an artistic and elitist will to shape matter. Jay's example here is the fascist adoption of this idea, as illustrated by Mussolini's comparison of the masses to wax in his hands. Whereas these two uses illustrate the dominance of art over life and artistic will over public, Jay identifies a third use, where aesthetics is associated with 'the seductive power of images'. This

form of aestheticised politics indicates 'the victory of the spectacle over the public sphere', where any potential for rational deliberation in public space is overwhelmed by images in a spell-binding yet illusionary spectacle (Jay 1992: 45). Jay (1992: 44) here notes Walter Benjamin's 'bitter observation that mankind's "self-alienation has reached such a degree that it can experience its own destruction as an aesthetic pleasure of the first order" ("Work of Art" 244) [which] vividly expresses the disgust aroused by this callous apotheosis of art over life'.

6. Jay's own examples are Arendt and Lyotard, both of whom were inspired by Kant's theory of aesthetic judgement in their understanding of politics/ethics while eschewing the sort of aestheticised politics that has been associated with fascism.

7. See, for example, the collection of essays in Wilson and Swyngedouw (2014).

8. As Bernstein (1986: 126), one of the harshest critics of Arendt's separation of the social from the political, writes, she 'helps us to overcome being mesmerized into thinking that politics occurs only in what is conventionally called "politics": in party bureaucracies, elections, the "power" of ruling cliques and interest groups . . . Arendt opens the space for thinking of politics in a radically different manner.'

Chapter 2

1. *Le goût des autres*, directed by Agnès Jaoui (Pathé 2000).

2. It is not my aim to cover the literature on various aesthetic theories of politics. For a sample, see Ferguson (2007: 133 n. 1).

3. To avoid a possible confusion, note that Kant wrote two introductions to the *Critique of Judgment*. The so-called 'First Introduction' was not published, but it is included in the Cambridge edition (Guyer and Matthews translation).

4. As Kant puts it elsewhere in the third Critique, 'the judgement of taste is merely contemplative, i.e., a judgement that, indifferent with regard to the existence of an object, merely connects its constitution together with the feeling of pleasure and displeasure. But this contemplation itself is also not directed to concepts; for the judgement of taste is not a cognitive judgement (neither a theoretical nor a practical one), and hence it is neither grounded on concepts nor aimed at them' (*CJ* §5).

5. Here it may be necessary to distinguish between aesthetic judgements and aesthetically grounded logical judgements. To use an example Kant gives, I may be looking at a rose and declare it to be beautiful. If, however, after having compared many roses, I then arrive at a judgement that 'roses in general are beautiful', this is no longer a

pure aesthetic judgement in the Kantian sense, but an 'aesthetically grounded logical judgement' (*CJ* §8), as I have subsumed all roses under a general rule.

6. Arendt here presents her own translation of part of §19 from Kant's *Critique of Judgment*. The section in the Guyer and Matthews translation reads: 'The judgment of taste ascribes assent to everyone, and whoever declares something to be beautiful wishes that everyone should approve of the object in question and similarly declare it to be beautiful. The should in aesthetic judgments of taste is thus pronounced only conditionally even given all the data that are required for the judging. One solicits assent from everyone else because one has a ground for it that is common to all.'

7. This is what Ferrara calls 'Kant's strategy of "naturalizing" sensus communis'. Kant 'tries to show that sensus communis, understood as a shared feeling, is presupposed by the very idea of the communicability of pleasure – a communicability that in turn can be seen as connected with the structure and interrelation of the imagination and the understanding, arguably shared by all human beings' (Ferrara 2008: 27, 28).

8. The term 'enlarged mentality' is Arendt's translation. This is given as a 'broadened' or 'broad-minded' way of thinking in the different English translations, in §40 where Kant discusses *sensus communis* and the universal communicability of aesthetic judgements.

9. This extract from Arendt's 1964 lecture at Chicago on 'Kant's political philosophy' is cited on pp. 141–2 of Beiner, 'Interpretive Essay', in Arendt (1992).

10. Another source of tension is that these 'two models' are guided by two different philosophical sources; the former (actor's standpoint) by Aristotle and the latter (spectator's standpoint) by Kant. See Passerin d'Entrèves (2000); see also Ferrara (2008) for an argument that these are not necessarily mutually inconsistent. Note that Arendt here is comparing Hegel and Kant. She notes that for the former the spectator exists in the singular, whereas for the latter spectators exist in the plural. Her own notion of spectatorship is informed by Kant's, whom she sees as 'more aware than any other philosopher of human plurality', with an emphasis on plurality, but this does not necessarily imply that she unconditionally subscribes to Kant's prioritisation of the spectator over the actor. As she puts it in her *Lectures on Kant's Political Philosophy*: 'We found that in Kant the common distinction or antagonism between theory and practice in political matters is the distinction between the spectator and the actor, and *to our surprise* we saw that the spectator had precedence: what counted in the French Revolution, what made it a world-historical event, a phenomenon not

to be forgotten, were not the deeds and misdeeds of the actors but the opinions, the enthusiastic approbation, of spectators, of persons who themselves were not involved. We also saw that these uninvolved and non-participating spectators . . . *were* involved with one another' (Arendt 1992: 65; emphasis added).

11. Note that the opening of the sentence is a direct allusion to Kant's notion of aesthetic (reflective) judgement, which he distinguishes, as we saw in the section 'Aesthetic Judgement and Common Sense', from determinative judgements in that the former operates, unlike the latter, without rules to subsume the particular under it. Arendt does not cite Kant here, but even the terms she uses come from his third Critique. This is important, because this essay, 'Understanding and Politics', was originally published in 1954, before Arendt outlined her ideas about action in *The Human Condition* in 1958.

12. For a different interpretation that suggests that, even though judgement was signalled earlier in Arendt's work, there was nevertheless a shift in emphasis on the judgement of the story-teller that somehow replaced the priority of action, see Beiner (1994); Hutchings (1996). Villa (2000: 17) also maintains that it is not 'plausible to suggest that Arendt came to abandon her stress on what Jerome Kohn calls "the priority of the political" in favour of a secular form of theodicy. It is better, I think, to view this phase of Arendt's work as an attempt to think through the tension between the life of the citizen and the life of the mind. In many respects, this tension occupied Arendt throughout her intellectual career.'

13. 'In point of fact', writes Arendt (2005: 169) elsewhere, 'the real political faculty in Kant's philosophy is not lawgiving reason, but judgement, which in an enlarged mentality has the power to override its "subjective private conditions".'

14. As Hutchings (1996: 94) notes, 'crucial to Arendt's concept of politics is a notion of human activity which is not structured by the violence of truth, morality or law'.

15. 'Were the common world ontologically given', Zerilli (2012: 22–3) observes, 'then it would be hard to see how it could ever be lost. But in Arendt's account it surely can. We do better to think of the common world as a political achievement, however rooted it may be in the ontological idea of human plurality.'

16. This is not to suggest that interruption as such is always politically desirable, a point I address in the previous chapter.

17. This 'challenge of equality' has been central to Rancière's thinking all along: 'But for all their variety, from the time of the break with Althusser, through his archival work and involvement with *Les Révoltes Logiques* to his most recent writings on politics, art and

literature, the unfolding of a single project can be clearly discerned. The consistency of Rancière's work is that of the repeated thrust of a single point, the challenge of equality, posed as a polemical intervention into two counter-posed domains, those of philosophy and history' (Thomson 2011: 200).

18. Rancière may also have been inspired by Joseph Jacotot, a French schoolteacher he encountered during his research in the archives. Exiled in the Netherlands, Jacotot caused quite a stir in nineteenth-century pedagogical debates when he claimed that all people had equal intelligence. His aim, however, was not proving empirically that all intelligence was equal; it was to see 'what can be done under that supposition' (Rancière 1991: 46). Even though Rancière had already started building his political thought before this encounter, he notes that what appealed to him in Jacotot was 'the radical manner in which [he] formulated the egalitarian idea' (Rancière 2004b: 222–3).

19. I am not using 'experience' in its technical, Kantian sense, as this would imply cognition. As Strawson (1991: 30; emphasis added) explains: 'Experience, empirical knowledge, is possible only when intuitions are *brought under concepts*, when empirical judgements are made . . . in the Transcendental Deduction . . . there is a general argument to the effect that the concepts under which we bring the contents of our experience must be such as to confer upon that experience a certain *rule-governed* connectedness or unity.' As aesthetic judgements are merely reflective, they are not determined by concepts, and they do not give rise to cognition; that is, they do not produce knowledge. Therefore, in strictly Kantian terms, 'aesthetic experience' would be a contradiction in terms.

20. See also Rancière (2004a: 13; 2007: 9; 2009b: 157).

Chapter 3

1. The second Pasqua law (the first one dates from 1986), named after the then-minister of the interior, restricted entry and residence rights of foreigners with a stated aim of 'zero immigration'. The majority of the occupiers were from West Africa (Mali, in particular, but also from Senegal, Mauritania and Guinea, all France's former colonies, part of French West Africa).

2. Madjiguène Cissé was part of the group that occupied Saint-Ambroise, and then Saint-Bernard churches. She was one of the spokespeople for the Saint-Bernard collective.

3. For an interpretation of undocumented immigrants in Western Europe through Arendt's notion of 'statelessness', see Krause (2008). For a different perspective, see Beltrán (2009), who follows Arendt as

a theorist of agonistic and performative politics in her interpretation
of the spring 2006 demonstrations against anti-immigrant legislation
and for immigrant rights in the United States for a reconsideration of
the 'undocumented'.
4. Reported at http://www.theguardian.com/global/blog/2011/jan/25/
middleeast-tunisia (accessed 1 May 2014).
5. Arendt characterises freedom in these terms in her other writings as
well. See, e.g., Arendt (2006: 23, 115).
6. The other strand that Marchart identifies in contradistinction to the
Arendtian one is the Schmittian, 'dissociative', strand where political
relation is one of antagonism.
7. As Bickford (1995: 320) observes: 'Our group identities may subject
us to stereotyped attention, but they are often also where we "draw
our strength to live and our reasons for acting" [quoting Simone de
Beauvoir]. Our colour, ethnicity, gender, class, or religion may be a
constitutive part of our public identity because they are the contexts in
which we learned to speak and think the languages that shape us and
enable us to give voice to our unique selves. And it is within particular
social groups that we first are paid attention to, and learn to attend to
others – the very capacities necessary for an Arendtian politics.'
8. This is why Lindahl (2006: 896) refers to Arendt's notion of space
of appearance as a sort of 'protospace', because 'spatial unity, as
founded in a legal order, leads back, both logically and chronologi-
cally, to a founding space . . . No legal institutionalisation of spatial
unity exhausts these protospaces.'
9. *The Origins of Totalitarianism* was originally published in 1951, and,
as Dietz (2000) notes, Arendt researched and published articles on the
totalitarian horrors of Nazism between 1945 and 1955.
10. However, Pitkin (1981: 341) also notes that 'nothing could be further
from Arendt's intentions. She explicitly disparaged trivial and vain
self-display . . . Despite indications to the contrary, Arendt really was
after self-development and not self-display; her goal was the "actualisation" or making "patent" of the actor's "latent self".'
11. The published English translation of this part reads: 'Politics can exist
only in the presence of a space in which human beings recognize
themselves as citizens, in which they situate one another within the
limits of a *common world*; and social life cannot exist in any true
sense unless human beings experience their mutual interdependence
solely as a result of the division of labour and of the necessity of
satisfying their needs' (Lefort 1988: 49). This is not consistent with
Arendt's argument. One way of correcting it would be to replace
'unless' with 'if', but still the translation seems to me inaccurate, so I
translate this sentence from the original.

12. As Canovan (1985: 620) puts it, 'Arendt's public realm, then, concerns a solid, durable common world, and constitutes something much more fragile and transitory, a space within which people act and appear in the presence of one another.' This is the space of appearance that comes into being from within the world of artefacts.
13. This is not, however, something Arendt objects to. As Bernstein (1986: 128 n. 5) observes, Arendt does recognise that 'social issues, including the question of poverty, can be transformed into political issues'.
14. As Arendt (1994: 23) put it in an interview, 'we start something. We weave our strand into a network of relations.'

Chapter 4

1. Throughout this chapter I refer to 'beings' to imply everything in existence and not just human beings. This is an aspect of Nancy's work that is different from Arendt's and Rancière's. Nancy's understanding of singular beings is not anthropocentric, which opens the way to thinking non-human politics, although this is not something I pursue in this book.
2. This is why James (2006) situates this understanding of space as a spatial and temporal unfolding that opens an intelligible world to Heidegger's account of primary spatiality in his *Being and Time*, and to the German phenomenological tradition more generally. Nancy seems to blend together elements from Heidegger and Husserl in developing his own account of space, spatiality and being, or 'rewriting', in James's words, the phenomenological account of space.
3. I am aware that Nancy does not have a clear and systematic political 'project'. As Kervégan (2004: 37) puts it, Nancy's politics remains 'lacunar'; even though there is a political concern manifest in his writings, he does not develop a 'political philosophy'.
4. This is a permanent possibility, and the way Nancy conceives of community constantly resists it: 'This is the coming to presence of *our* freedom, the common experience of the exposure in which the community is founded, but founded only through and for an infinite resistance to every appropriation of the essence, collective or individual, of its sharing, or of its foundation' (Nancy 1993: 95).
5. As Morin (2012: 114) also observes: 'Nancy is much more careful in *The Truth of Democracy* to delineate the sphere of the in-common as the sphere of sense-making against the sphere of the political.'

Chapter 5

1. From Éric Rochant's 1997 movie *Vive la République!*
2. This interpretation was first formulated in Dikeç (2007).

3. 'The political intervention', writes Rancière (1994: 176), 'is that which designates as the manifestation of a *logos* what in the police order is seen only as noise.'

4. Rancière's original formulation is 'son propre espace'. The term *propre* in this context does not mean 'proper' but 'own'. See Rancière (1998: 177, Thèse 8).

5. In English the term may sound more pejorative than it does in French. The first meaning of *la police* given in *Le Petit Robert* dictionary is 'government, organization'. Another example may be Microsoft Word. The option 'Font', which is about ordering and organising the way the text looks, is called 'Police' in the French version.

6. Rancière plays on the word 'wrong' (*le tort*), which comes from the verb *tordre*, to twist.

7. See note 4 above for the modification of translation.

8. Rancière's premise here is that another police order will eventually be established. It might be useful to note that the police does not refer to a transcendental order, but to any hierarchical structure.

9. Such an argument challenges rational and procedural positions. Rancière criticises, for example, Habermas, for he presupposes 'that both the interlocutors and the objects about which they speak are preconstituted'. According to Rancière (2000c: 116), however, 'there can be political exchange only when there is not such a preestablished agreement – not only, that is, regarding the objects of debate but also regarding the status of the speakers themselves'.

10. The centrality of equality allows Rancière to distinguish his politics from other forms of dissensus – for example, extreme right movements, which are not motivated by the verification of the equality of anyone with anyone. He writes: 'I do not reduce politics to a mere agonistic schema where the "content" is irrelevant ... Politics, I argue, has its own universal, its own measure that is equality. The measure never applies directly. It does so only through the enactment of a wrong. However, not every wrong is necessarily political. It has been argued against my theses that there are also anti-democratic forms of protest among the oppressed, shaped by religious fanaticism or ethnic identitarianism and intolerance. Ernesto Laclau ... put this as the blind spot of my conceptualisation of dissensus ... But it is clear that in my view a wrong is political when it enacts the basis of political action, which is the mere contingency of equality, which is evidently not the case of "popular" movements asking for the purity of the blood, the power of religion, and so on' (Rancière 2011a: 4).

11. In the English translation, this part is given as 'a place's destination'. 'Function', I believe, would be a more appropriate translation, which is what is implied in the phrase 'la destination d'un lieu'.

12. These, of course, are not the only spatial terms in Rancière's work, but the ones that are central to his conceptualisation and differentiation of politics and the police. His writings are rich with others such as division, distribution, partition, transgression, displacement, and so on.

13. 'As conceived by "the police", society is a totality comprised of groups performing specific functions and occupying determined spaces' (Rancière 2000c: 124). Note, however, that this interview was conducted in French. I have tried to locate the original transcription to check the precise term used by Rancière, but it was not available at the time of writing.

14. As in *chacun à sa place* ('each to his/her proper place, the place where s/he belongs'), or *savoir rester à sa place* ('to know one's place').

15. The French *place* comes from the Latin *platea*. The more technical term *platée* is also derived from *platea*, and means 'foundation of a building'.

16. This raises the question of whether Rancière is after some form of pure politics that occurs only rarely. Indeed, he wrote in *Disagreement* that 'politics, in its specificity, is rare' (Rancière 1999: 139). Since then, however, he seems to have recognised this as a problem. Asked about his earlier statement about the rarity of politics, he says that 'today [he] would certainly re-consider' (Rancière 2009e: 181).

17. This interview was first published in English in 2003, where the quoted part is translated as the following: 'However, all my work on workers' emancipation showed that the most prominent of the claims put forward by the workers and the poor was precisely the claim to visibility, a will to enter the political realm of appearance, the affirmation of a capacity for appearance' (Rancière 2003a: 202). It strikes me as contradictory for Rancière to criticise Arendt for distinguishing between a political and a social realm, and then to talk about 'a will to enter the *political* realm of appearance'. This adjective does not appear in the French version of this interview, revised by Rancière and published in 2009 in a collection of interviews (see Rancière 2009d: 341).

18. That said, it is important to note that place-making does not inherently imply emancipatory politics; it could, indeed, work against it, as in fascist regimes and various forms of fundamentalism (Euben 2002; Kohn 2003). Emancipatory politics are committed to the postulate of radical equality; that is, the equality of anyone with anyone.

Chapter 6

1. Note that the 'free play' occasioned by the beautiful already suggests a dissensus for Rancière, as he explains in his critique of Lyotard: 'In itself, the "free agreement" between understanding and the

imagination is already in itself a disagreement or dissensus. It is not necessary to go looking in the sublime experience of size, power or fear to discern a disagreement between thought and the sensible or to ground modern art's radicality in the play of attraction and repulsion' (Rancière 2009c: 97).

2. This is also the basis of Rancière's critique (2004d; 2009c) of Lyotard. He is critical of the use Lyotard makes of the sublime, not of the sublime as such. In his view, Lyotard is guilty of turning the aesthetics of the sublime into an ethics, of transforming sublime unrepresentability into an ethical imperative of absolute respect for otherness.

Bibliography

Allison, E. Henry (2001), *Kant's Theory of Taste: A Reading of the Critique of Aesthetic Judgment*, Cambridge: Cambridge University Press.

Arditi, Benjamin (2007), *Politics on the Edges of Liberalism: Difference, Populism, Revolution, Agitation*, Edinburgh: Edinburgh University Press.

Arendt, Hannah (1958), *The Human Condition*, Chicago: University of Chicago Press.

Arendt, Hannah (1968) [1951], *The Origins of Totalitarianism,* Orlando: Harcourt, Inc.

Arendt, Hannah (1977), *Between Past and Future*, New York: Penguin Books.

Arendt, Hannah (1978), *The Life of the Mind*, vol. I. *Thinking*, vol. II. *Willing*, New York: Harcourt Brace Jovanovich.

Arendt, Hannah (1987), 'Labor, work, action', in J. W. Bernauer (ed.), *Amor Mundi: Explorations in the Faith and Thought of Hannah Arendt*, Dordrecht: Martinus Nijhoff, 29–42.

Arendt, Hannah (1992), *Lectures on Kant's Political Philosophy*, ed. R. Beiner, Chicago: University of Chicago Press.

Arendt, Hannah (1994), *Essays in Understanding, 1930–1954: Formation, Exile, Totalitarianism*, ed. J. Kohn, New York: Schocken Books.

Arendt, Hannah (2005), *The Promise of Politics*, ed. J. Kohn, New York: Schocken Books.

Arendt, Hannah (2006), *On Revolution*, New York: Penguin Books.

Beiner, Ronald (1992), 'Interpretive essay: Hannah Arendt on judging', in H. Arendt, *Lectures on Kant's Political Philosophy*, Chicago: University of Chicago Press, 87–156.

Beiner, Ronald (1994), 'Judging in a world of appearances', in L. Hinchman and S. Hinchman (eds), *Hannah Arendt: Critical Essays*, Albany: State University of New York Press, 365–88.

Beiner, Ronald, and Nedelsky, Jennifer (2001), 'Introduction', in R. Beiner and J. Nedelsky (eds), *Judgment, Imagination, and Politics: Themes from Kant and Arendt*, Lanham, MD: Rowman & Littlefield, vii–xxvi.

Beltrán, Cristina (2009), 'Going public: Hannah Arendt, immigrant action, and the space of appearance', *Political Theory*, 37(5): 595–622.

Benveniste, Emile (1969), *Le vocabulaire des institutions indo-européennes, Tome II: Pouvoir, droit, religion*, Paris: Les Éditions de Minuit.

Bernstein, J. Richard (1986), 'Rethinking the social and the political', *Graduate Faculty Philosophy Journal*, 11(1): 111–30.

Bickford, Susan (1995), 'In the presence of others: Arendt and Anzaldúa on the paradox of public appearance', in B. Honig (ed.), *Feminist Interpretations of Hannah Arendt*, University Park: Pennsylvania State University Press, 313–35.

Bowie, Andrew (2003), *Aesthetics and Subjectivity: From Kant to Nietzsche*, 2nd edn, Manchester: Manchester University Press.

Buckler, Steve (2011), *Hannah Arendt and Political Theory: Challenging the Tradition*, Edinburgh: Edinburgh University Press.

Burke, Edmund (1998) [1757], *A Philosophical Enquiry into the Origin of our Ideas of the Sublime and Beautiful and Other Pre-Revolutionary Writings*, ed. D. Womersley, London: Penguin Books.

Canovan, Margaret (1985), 'Politics as culture', *History of Political Thought*, 6(3): 617–42.

Cascardi, Anthony (1997), 'Communication and transformation: Aesthetics and politics in Kant and Arendt', in C. Calhoun and J. McGowan (eds), *Hannah Arendt and the Meaning of Politics*, Minneapolis: University of Minnesota Press, 99–131.

Casey, Edward (1997), *The Fate of Place: A Philosophical History*, Berkeley: University of California Press.

Caygill, Howard (1997), 'The shared world: philosophy, violence, freedom', in D. Sheppard, S. Sparks and C. Thomas (eds), *The Sense of Philosophy: On Jean-Luc Nancy*, London: Routledge, 19–31.

Cissé, Madjiguène (1999), *Parole de sans-papiers*, Paris: La Dispute.

Cissé, Madjiguène (2007), 'Emigration choisie: entretien avec Madjiguène Cissé', *Vacarme*, 38 <http://www.vacarme.org/article1230.html> (accessed 8 July 2011).

Critchley, Simon (1999a), *Ethics, Politics, Subjectivity: Essays on Derrida, Levinas and Contemporary French Thought*, London: Verso.

Critchley, Simon (1999b), *The Ethics of Deconstruction: Derrida and Levinas*, Edinburgh: Edinburgh University Press.

Curtis, Kimberley (1997), 'Aesthetic foundations of democratic politics in the work of Hannah Arendt', in C. Calhoun and J. McGowan (eds), *Hannah Arendt and the Meaning of Politics*, Minneapolis: University of Minnesota Press, 27–52.

Dallmayr, Fred (1997), 'An "inoperative" global community? Reflections on Nancy', in D. Sheppard, S. Sparks and C. Thomas (eds), *The Sense of Philosophy: On Jean-Luc Nancy*, London: Routledge, 174–96.

Deleuze, Gilles (1978a), Kant lecture of 28 March, trans. Melissa McMahon <http://www.webdeleuze.com/php/sommaire.html> (accessed 8 June 2014).

Deleuze, Gilles (1978b), Kant lecture of 4 April, trans. Melissa McMahon <http://www.webdeleuze.com/php/sommaire.html> (accessed 8 June 2014).

Deleuze, Gilles (2008), *Kant's Critical Philosophy*, London: Continuum.

Deranty, Jean-Philippe (2003), 'Jacques Rancière's contribution to the ethics of recognition', *Political Theory*, 31(1): 136–56.

Deranty, Jean-Philippe, and Renault, Emmanuel (2009), 'Democratic agon: Striving for distinction or struggle against domination and injustice?', in A. Schaap (ed.), *Law and Agonistic Politics*, Farnham: Ashgate, 43–56.

Devisch, Ignaas (2000), 'A trembling voice in the desert: Jean-Luc Nancy's rethinking of the space of the political', *Cultural Values*, 4(2): 239–56.

Dietz, G. Mary (2000), 'Arendt and the Holocaust', in D. Villa (ed.), *The Cambridge Companion to Hannah Arendt*, Cambridge: Cambridge University Press, 86–110.

Dikeç, Mustafa (2007), *Badlands of the Republic: Space, Politics and Urban Policy*, London: Blackwell.

Dikeç, Mustafa (2012), 'Space as a mode of political thinking', *Geoforum*, 43(4): 669–76.

Dikeç, Mustafa (forthcoming), *Urban Rage*, New Haven: Yale University Press.

Eagleton, Terry (1990), *The Ideology of the Aesthetic*, Oxford: Basil Blackwell.

Euben, J. Peter (2002), 'The polis, globalization, and the politics of place', in A. Botwinick and W. E. Connolly (eds), *Democracy and Vision: Sheldon Wolin and the Vicissitudes of the Political*, Princeton: Princeton University Press, 256–89.

Featherstone, David (2008), *Resistance, Space and Political Identities: The Making of Counter-Global Networks*, London: Blackwell.

Ferguson, Kennan (2007), *The Politics of Judgement: Aesthetics, Identity, and Political Theory*, Lanham, MD: Lexington Books.

Ferrara, Alessandro (2008), *The Force of the Example: Explorations in the Paradigm of Judgment*, New York: Columbia University Press.

Fraser, Nancy (1997), 'Communication, transformation, and consciousness-raising', in C. Calhoun and J. McGowan (eds), *Hannah Arendt and the Meaning of Politics*, Minneapolis: University of Minnesota Press, 166–75.

Fynsk, Christopher (1991), 'Experiences of finitude', Foreword to J.-L. Nancy, *The Inoperative Community*, Minneapolis: University of Minnesota Press, vii–xxxv.

Gasché, Rodolphe (2003), *The Idea of Form: Rethinking Kant's Aesthetics*, Stanford: Stanford University Press.

Gregory, Derek (1994), *Geographical Imaginations*, Oxford: Blackwell.

Guyer, Paul (1996), *Kant and the Experience of Freedom*, Cambridge: Cambridge University Press.

Harvey, David (2000), *Spaces of Hope*, Berkeley: University of California Press.

Heidegger, Martin (1962), *Being and Time*, Oxford: Blackwell.

Henrich, Dieter (1992), *Aesthetic Judgement and the Moral Image of the World: Studies in Kant*, Stanford: Stanford University Press.

Honig, Bonnie (1993), *Political Theory and the Displacement of Politics*, Ithaca, NY: Cornell University Press.

Honig, Bonnie (1995), 'Towards an agonistic feminism: Hannah Arendt and the politics of identity', in B. Honig (ed.), *Feminist Interpretations of Hannah Arendt*, University Park: Pennsylvania State University Press, 135–66.

Hughes, Fiona (2010), *Kant's Critique of Aesthetic Judgement*, London: Continuum.

Hume, David (2008), *Selected Essays*, ed. S. Copley and A. Edgar, Oxford: Oxford University Press.

Husserl, Edmund (1997), *Thing and Space: Lectures of 1907*, Dordrecht: Kluwer Academic Publishers.

Hutchings, Kimberly (1996), *Kant, Critique and Politics*, London: Routledge.

Ingram, D. James (2007), 'The subject of the politics of recognition: Hannah Arendt and Jacques Rancière', in G. W. Bertram et al. (eds), *Socialité et reconnaissance: grammaires de l'humain*, Paris: L'Harmattan, 229–45.

Isin, Engin (2002), *Being Political: Genealogies of Citizenship*, Minneapolis: University of Minnesota Press.

James, Ian (2006), *The Fragmentary Demand: An Introduction to the Philosophy of Jean-Luc Nancy*, Stanford: Stanford University Press.

Jay, Martin (1992), '"The aesthetic ideology" as ideology: Or, what does it mean to aestheticize politics?', *Cultural Critique*, 21: 41–61.

Jay, Martin (1997), 'Reflective judgments by a spectator on a conference that is now history', in C. Calhoun and J. McGowan (eds), *Hannah Arendt and the Meaning of Politics*, Minneapolis: University of Minnesota Press, 338–50.

Kalyvas, Andreas (2008), *Democracy and the Politics of the Extraordinary: Max Weber, Carl Schmitt, and Hannah Arendt*, Cambridge: Cambridge University Press.

Kant, Immanuel (1997) [1788], *Critique of Practical Reason*, trans. and ed. M. Gregor, Cambridge: Cambridge University Press.

Kant, Immanuel (1998) [1781], *Critique of Pure Reason*, trans. and ed. P. Guyer and A. W. Wood, Cambridge: Cambridge University Press.

Kant, Immanuel (2000) [1790], *Critique of the Power of Judgment*, trans. P. Guyer and E. Matthews, Cambridge: Cambridge University Press.

Kateb, George (2001), 'The judgement of Arendt', in R. Beiner and J. Nedelsky (eds), *Judgment, Imagination, and Politics: Themes from Kant and Arendt*, Lanham, MD: Rowman & Littlefield Publishers, 121–38.

Kateb, George (2006), 'Political action: Its nature and advantages', in D. Villa (ed.), *The Cambridge Companion to Hannah Arendt*, Cambridge: Cambridge University Press, 130–48.

Keith, Michael, and Pile, Steve (1993), *Place and the Politics of Identity*, London: Routledge.

Kervégan, Jean-François (2004), 'Un hégélianisme sans profondeur', in F. Guibal and J.-C. Martin (eds), *Sens en tous sens: autour des travaux de Jean-Luc Nancy*, Paris: Galilée, 25–37.

Kohn, Margaret (2003), *Radical Space: Building the House of the People*, Ithaca, NY: Cornell University Press.

Krause, Monika (2008), 'Undocumented migrants: An Arendtian perspective', *European Journal of Political Theory*, 7: 331–48.

Laclau, Ernesto, and Mouffe, Chantal (1985), *Hegemony and Socialist Strategy: Towards a Radical Democratic Politics*, London: Verso.

Lacoue-Labarthe, Philippe, and Nancy, Jean-Luc (1997), *Retreating the Political*, London: Routledge.

Le Monde (2002), 'Le ministre veut publier plus fréquemment les chiffres de la délinquance', *Le Monde*, 31 May.

Lefebvre, Henri (1977), 'Reflections on the politics of space', in R. Peet (ed.), *Radical Geography: Alternative Viewpoints on Contemporary Social Issues*, Chicago: Maaroufa Press, 339–52.

Lefebvre, Henri (1991) [1974], *The Production of Space*, Oxford: Blackwell.

Lefort, Claude (1986), *Essais sur le politique*, Paris: Seuil.

Lefort, Claude (1988), *Democracy and Political Theory*, Minneapolis: University of Minnesota Press.

Lindahl, Hans (2006), 'Give and take: Arendt and the *nomos* of political community', *Philosophy and Social Criticism*, 32(7): 881–901.

McClure, Kirstie (1997), 'The odor of judgment: Exemplarity, propriety, and politics in the company of Hannah Arendt', in C. Calhoun and J. McGowan (eds), *Hannah Arendt and the Meaning of Politics*, Minneapolis: University of Minnesota Press, 53–84.

Malpas, Jeff (2012), 'Putting space in place: Philosophical topography and relational geography', *Environment and Planning D: Society and Space*, 30(2): 226–42.

Manchev, Boyan (2012), 'La matière du monde et l'*aisthesis* du common', in G. Berkman and D. Cohen-Levinas (eds), *Figures du dehors: autour de Jean-Luc Nancy*, Nantes: Editions Cécile Defaut, 375–91.

Marchart, Oliver (2007), *Post-Foundational Political Thought: Political Difference in Nancy, Lefort, Badiou and Laclau*, Edinburgh: Edinburgh University Press.

Markell, Patchen (2010), 'The rule of the people: Arendt, *archê*, and democracy', in S. Benhabib (ed.), *Politics in Dark Times: Encounters with Hannah Arendt*, Cambridge: Cambridge University Press, 58–82.

Markell, Patchen (2011), 'Arendt's work: On the architecture of *The Human Condition*', *College Literature*, 38(1): 15–44.

Massey, Doreen (1993), 'Politics and space/time', in M. Keith and S. Pile (eds), *Place and the Politics of Identity*, London: Routledge, 141–61.

Massey, Doreen (1999), 'Spaces of politics', in D. Massey, J. Allen and P. Sarre (eds), *Human Geography Today*, Cambridge: Polity Press, 279–94.

Massey, Doreen (2005), *For Space*, London: Sage.

Mitchell, W. J. T. (2013), 'Image, space, revolution', in W. J. T. Mitchell, B. E. Harcourt and M. Taussig, *Occupy: Three Inquiries in Disobedience*, Chicago: University of Chicago Press, 93–130.

Morin, Marie-Eve (2012), *Jean-Luc Nancy*, Cambridge: Polity.

Nancy, Jean-Luc (1991), *The Inoperative Community*, Minneapolis: University of Minnesota Press.

Nancy, Jean-Luc (1993), *The Experience of Freedom*, Stanford: Stanford University Press.

Nancy, Jean-Luc (1997), *The Sense of the World*, Minneapolis: University of Minnesota Press.

Nancy, Jean-Luc (2000a), *Being Singular Plural*, Stanford: Stanford University Press.

Nancy, Jean-Luc (2000b), 'Rien que le monde: entretien avec Jean-Luc Nancy', *Vacarme*, 11, 2 April <http://www.vacarme.org/article442.html> (accessed 13 September 2014).

Nancy, Jean-Luc (2001), *La pensée dérobée*, Paris: Galilée.

Nancy, Jean-Luc (2002), 'Is everything political?', *CR: The New Centennial Review*, 2(3): 15–22.

Nancy, Jean-Luc (2003), *A Finite Thinking*, ed. S. Sparks, Stanford: Stanford University Press.

Nancy, Jean-Luc (2007), *The Creation of the World or Globalization*, Albany: State University of New York Press.

Nancy, Jean-Luc (2008), *Vérité de la démocratie*, Paris: Galilée.

Nancy, Jean-Luc (2011), *Politique et au-delà*, Paris: Galilée.

Nancy, Jean-Luc (2013), *La possibilité d'un monde*, Paris: Les petits Platons.

Panagia, Davide (2006), *The Poetics of Political Thinking*, Durham, NC: Duke University Press.

Panagia, Davide (2009), *The Political Life of Sensation*, Durham, NC: Duke University Press.

Passerin d'Entrèves, Maurizio (2000), 'Arendt's theory of judgment', in D. Villa (ed.), *The Cambridge Companion to Hannah Arendt*, Cambridge: Cambridge University Press, 245–60.

Pitkin, F. Hannah (1981), 'Justice: On relating private and public', *Political Theory*, 9(3): 327–52.

Rancière, Jacques (1989) [1981], *The Nights of Labor: The Workers' Dream in Nineteenth-Century France*, Philadelphia: Temple University Press.

Rancière, Jacques (1991) [1987], *The Ignorant Schoolmaster: Five Lessons in Intellectual Emancipation*, Stanford: Stanford University Press.

Rancière, Jacques (1994), 'Post-democracy, politics and philosophy: An interview with Jacques Rancière, *Angelaki*, 1(3): 171–8.

Rancière, Jacques (1995a), *On the Shores of Politics*, London: Verso.

Rancière, Jacques (1995b), 'Politics, identification, and subjectivization', in J. Rajchman (ed.), *The Identity in Question*, New York: Routledge, 63–70.

Rancière, Jacques (1997), 'Democracy means equality' (interview), *Radical Philosophy*, 82: 29–36.

Rancière, Jacques (1998), *Aux bords du politique*, rev. edn, Paris: La Fabrique.

Rancière, Jacques (1999) [1995], *Disagreement: Politics and Philosophy*, Minneapolis: University of Minnesota Press.

Rancière, Jacques (2000a), 'Jacques Rancière: Literature, politics, aesthetics' (interviewed by Solange Guénoun and James H. Kavanagh), *SubStance*, 29(2): 3–24.

Rancière, Jacques (2000b), *Le partage du sensible: esthétique et politique*, Paris: La Fabrique.

Rancière, Jacques (2000c), 'Dissenting words: A conversation with Jacques Rancière', *diacritics*, 30(2): 113–26.

Rancière, Jacques (2000d), 'Biopolitique ou politique?' (interview), *Multitudes* (1) <http://www.cythere-critique.com/PRESSE/documents/ranciere.pdf> (accessed 23 May 2014).

Rancière, Jacques (2001), 'Ten theses on politics', *Theory & Event*, 5(3) <http://muse.jhu.edu/journals/theory_&_event/> (accessed 23 May 2014).

Rancière, Jacques (2003a), 'Politics and aesthetics: An interview', *Angelaki*, 8(2): 191–211.

Rancière, Jacques (2003b), 'The thinking of dissensus: Politics and aesthetics', paper presented at the conference 'Fidelity to the Disagreement: Jacques Rancière and the Political', Goldsmiths College, London, 16–17 September 2003.

Rancière, Jacques (2004a), *The Politics of Aesthetics*, London: Continuum.

Rancière, Jacques (2004b) [1983], *The Philosopher and His Poor*, Durham, NC: Duke University Press.

Rancière, Jacques (2004c), 'Who is the subject of the rights of man?', *South Atlantic Quarterly*, 103(2/3): 297–310.

Rancière, Jacques (2004d), 'The sublime from Lyotard to Schiller: Two readings of Kant and their political significance', *Radical Philosophy*, 126 (July/August): 8–15.

Rancière, Jacques (2005), 'From politics to aesthetics?', *Paragraph*, 28(1): 13–25.

Rancière, Jacques (2006), 'Thinking between disciplines: An aesthetics of knowledge', *Parrhesia*, 1: 1–12.

Rancière, Jacques (2007), 'Les territoires de la pensée partagée', interview with J. Lévy, J. Rennes and D. Zerbib, *EspacesTemps.net* <http://www.espacestemps.net/articles/jacques-ranciere-les-territoires-de-la-pensee-partagee/> (accessed 13 September 2014).

Rancière, Jacques (2009a), 'Contemporary art and the politics of aesthetics', in B. Hinderliter et al. (eds), *Communities of Sense: Rethinking Aesthetics and Politics*, Durham, NC: Duke University Press, 31–50.

Rancière, Jacques (2009b), 'Politique de l'indétermination esthétique', in J. Game and A. W. Lasowski (eds), *Jacques Rancière et la politique de l'esthétique*, Paris: Éditions des archives contemporaines, 157–75.

Rancière, Jacques (2009c), *Aesthetics and its Discontents*, Cambridge: Polity.

Rancière, Jacques (2009d), *Et tant pis pour les gens fatigués: entretiens*, Paris: Éditions Amsterdam.

Rancière, Jacques (2009e), *Moments politiques: interventions 1977–2009*, Paris: La Fabrique.

Rancière, Jacques (2011a), 'The thinking of dissensus: Politics and aesthetics', in P. Bowman and R. Stamp (eds), *Reading Rancière*, London: Continuum, 1–17.

Rancière, Jacques (2011b) [1974], *La leçon d'Althusser*, Paris: La Fabrique.

Rancière, Jacques (2012), *Jacques Rancière: la méthode de l'égalité*, Montrouge: Bayard.

Ross, Alison (2007), *The Aesthetic Paths of Philosophy: Presentation in Kant, Heidegger, Lacoue-Labarthe, and Nancy*, Stanford: Stanford University Press.

Ross, Kristin (2009), 'Historicizing untimeliness', in G. Rockhill and P. Watts (eds), *Jacques Rancière: History, Politics, Aesthetics*, Durham, NC: Duke University Press, 15–29.

Schaap, Andrew (2011), 'Enacting the right to have rights: Jacques Rancière's critique of Hannah Arendt', *European Journal of Political Theory*, 10(1): 22–45.

Schiller, Friedrich (2004) [1795], *On the Aesthetic Education of Man*, New York: Dover Publications.

Shapiro, Michael (2006), 'The sublime today: Re-partitioning the global sensible', *Millennium: Journal of International Studies*, 34(3): 657–81.

Siméant, Johanna (1998), *La cause des sans-papiers*, Paris: Presses de Sciences Po.

Smith, Neil (1990), *Uneven Development: Nature, Capital and the Production of Space*, Oxford: Blackwell.

Soja, Edward (1989), *Postmodern Geographies: The Reassertion of Space in Critical Social Theory*, London: Verso.

Strawson, Peter (1991), *The Bounds of Sense: As Essay on Kant's Critique of Pure Reason*, London: Routledge.

Taminiaux, Jacques (1997), *The Thracian Maid and the Professional Thinker: Arendt and Heidegger*, Albany: State University of New York Press.

Thomson, Alex (2011), 'On the shores of history', in P. Bowman and R. Stamp (eds), *Reading Rancière*, London: Continuum, 200–16.

Villa, R. Dana (2000), 'Introduction: The development of Arendt's political thought', in D. R. Villa (ed.), *The Cambridge Companion to Hannah Arendt*, Cambridge: Cambridge University Press, 1–21.

Villa, R. Dana (2001), 'Hannah Arendt: Modernity, alienation, and critique', in R. Beiner and J. Nedelsky (eds), *Judgment, Imagination, and Politics: Themes from Kant and Arendt*, Lanham, MD: Rowman & Littlefield Publishers, 287–310.

Wellmer, Albrecht (1997), 'Hannah Arendt on judgment: The unwritten doctrine of reason', in L. May and J. Kohn (eds), *Hannah Arendt: Twenty Years Later*, Cambridge, MA: MIT Press, 33–52.

Wilson, Japhy, and Swyngedouw, Erik (2014) (eds), *The Post-Political and its Discontents: Spaces of Depoliticisation, Spectres of Radical Politics*, Edinburgh: Edinburgh University Press.

Wolin, Sheldon (2004) [1960], *Politics and Vision: Continuity and Innovation in Western Political Thought*, Princeton: Princeton University Press.

Zerilli, Linda (2005), *Feminism and the Abyss of Freedom*, Chicago: University of Chicago Press.

Zerilli, Linda (2012), 'Value pluralism and the problem of judgment: Farewell to public reason', *Political Theory*, 40(1): 6–31.

Index

EU representative:
Easy Access System Europe
Mustamäe tee 50, 10621 Tallinn, Estonia
Gpsr.requests@easproject.com

www.ingramcontent.com/pod-product-compliance
Lightning Source LLC
Chambersburg PA
CBHW070346270326
41926CB00017B/4015